EVERYTHING YOU CAN DO
IN THE GARDEN
WITHOUT
ACTUALLY
GARDENING

EVERYTHING YOU CAN DO *IN THE GARDEN* WITHOUT ACTUALLY GARDENING

PHILIPPA LEWIS

FRANCES LINCOLN LIMITED
PUBLISHERS

For my mother, Diana Lewis

Frances Lincoln Ltd
4 Torriano Mews
Torriano Avenue
London NW5 2RZ
www.franceslincoln.com

Everything you Can Do in the Garden Without Actually Gardening
Copyright © Frances Lincoln 2009
Text copyright © Philippa Lewis 2009 and as acknowledged on page 210
Illustrations copyright © as acknowledged on page 7

First Frances Lincoln edition: 2009

A catalogue record for this book is available from the British Library.

ISBN 9-780-7112-3037-8

Printed and bound in Hong Kong

1 2 3 4 5 6 7 8 9

CONTENTS

ACKNOWLEDGMENTS

A book of allsorts such as this is comes into being with the help of numerous conversations and memories. Its present form was the result of fruitful discussion with Jaqueline Mitchell, but I owe this publication to Jo Christian of Frances Lincoln, who immediately saw the point.

Many people have been generous with their enthusiasm for the project and spent time retrieving and passing on quotations and references to me; I am immensely grateful to them. Julia Brown, Caroline Chapman, Martin and Liz Drury, Juliet Gardiner, Jenny Hartley, Mary Keen, David and Simone Sekers, Bettina Tayleur and Alister Warman all made imaginative contributions – as did Gillian Darley, who in addition took time to make invaluable comment on improving the text. Nicola Beauman encouraged me to do the initial research on the history of sitting in the garden.

Amoret Tanner's unsurpassed ephemera collection has provided some wonderful illustrations, but also her generous loan of original material allowed me to accumulate incidental detail impossible to find elsewhere.

John Bennett of *Fireworks* magazine was equally generous in providing his personal memoir as well as pictures. I should also like to thank Tom Fort and Posy Simmonds for permission to reproduce their work and enrich the book; and Todd Longstaffe-Gowan for letting me include a watercolour from his collection. Helen O'Neill at the London Library was particularly helpful in providing scans of problematical plates from books in the library, and as usual its shelves threw up much that I could not have possibly have come across elsewhere. It was a pleasure to be edited by Anne Askwith and I was encouraged by her enthusiasm. Arianna Osti reminded me how enjoyable it is to work with book designers.

Families are always mentioned last, but are the most important helpmeets. I have dedicated this book to my mother, Diana Lewis, who brought me up to love being out in the garden. My children, Tom, Hannah and Ned Thistlethwaite, have been boundlessly keen and supportive. My husband, Miles Thistlethwaite, has, as ever, been there reassuring me that what I am doing is worthwhile, making perceptive comments and asking the right questions.

Philippa Lewis, 2009

PICTURE CREDITS

listed by page number

A painting by Donald Towner of his neighbour's daughter, Alice Ashley,
sitting on a swing seat in a Hampstead garden, 1937.

INTRODUCTION

Ewbank'd inside and Atco'd out, the English suburban residence and the garden which is an integral part of it stand trim and lovingly cared for in the mild sunshine. Everything is in its place. The abruptness, the barbarities of the world are far away. There is not much sound, except perhaps the musical whirr and clack of a mowing machine being pushed back and forth over a neighbouring lawn and the clink of cups and saucers and a soft footfall as tea is got ready indoors. There is not much movement either: a wire-haired terrier lazily trotting round the garden in a not very hopeful search for something new to smell, and the pages of a newspaper being turned and refolded by some leisurely individual in a deck chair. It is an almost windless day.

(J.M. Richards, *The Castles on the Ground*, 1973)

This evocation of a garden, perhaps a Saturday afternoon in June, captures the peace and sense of detachment from the world that can exist in our private Edens. We can't return to a prelapsarian existence, but we can suspend our disbelief for a while. Within the garden we can create our own kingdoms and do precisely what we want.

So a clear boundary to the garden is important. Words on the subject echo down the centuries, from the Tudor poet and divine George Herbert's admonition 'Love your neighbour, yet pull not down your fences' to William Morris's advice (in his essay 'Hopes and Fears for Art', 1882) that the garden 'should be well fenced from the outside world'. Fences, walls and hedges allow us our privacy, even if section 6 of the Anti-Social Behaviour Act of 2003 now limits the leylandii from reaching its natural height of a hundred feet.

Once our surroundings are secure, what we do is up to us: the garden is our own world. The notion of what exactly constitutes a garden is endlessly various, as anyone staring out of a train window at a passing string of back gardens notices. The actual gardening is one large part of having a garden, but what do we do when that is done – or not done? How do we spend time in the garden and what do we value it for? Humans don't change much, so the pleasures are perennial: relief at the arrival of spring, sounds of birds, autumn bonfires, hoar frost, sky at night, smell of wet earth, feeling of sun warming our backbones or the flickering of light and shade. Out of doors we seek solitude and company, fresh air and exercise; we note the seasons and the weather; we might play games, make love, talk, eat, unwind, drink, read, let children loose and keep animals – just as we always have done.

A garden also provides a space for eccentricity. When Sir William Temple signed his will in 1694, he stated that while his body could lie in Westminster Abbey, he wanted his heart to be 'interred six foot underground on the South East side of the stone dyal in my little garden at Moreparke'. It was, buried in a china bowl. John Aubrey wrote in his *Brief Lives* (which he compiled at the end of the seventeenth century) notes on his friend and acquaintance Sir John Danvers, who had a garden in Chelsea, where he 'was wont in

The 1950s nuclear family enjoy a picnic tea on an immaculate lawn: illustration from a booklet, 'Garden for your Family', produced to advertise ICI weedkiller.

fair mornings in the summer to brush his Beaver-hatt on the Hysop and Thyme, which did perfume it with its natural Spirit; and would last a morning or longer'. William Blake's early biographer, Alexander Gilchrist, recounts a story (published in 1863) of how Blake's friend and patron Thomas Butts found Blake and his wife Catherine naked ('freed from the troublesome disguises which have prevailed since the Fall'), reciting passages from Milton's *Paradise Lost* to each other in the summer house of their Lambeth garden. In the early nineteenth century a George Durant of Tong Castle inserted a pulpit into his garden wall that enabled him to preach randomly at passersby – which must have been tiresome for the villagers, among whom were many of his illegitimate children, marked by him with whimsical names, Cinderella and Napoleon for two. Major Walter

Wingfield enjoyed shooting with a revolver from his bicycle in the garden. The target was a cardboard Turk's head stuck on a post: 'Considering the crisis in the East, this is good practice' (the year was 1896). Twentieth-century bearers of the eccentricity flame include Ann Atkins with her gnome reserve for over a thousand in Devon, and John Fairnington with his *jardin imaginaire*, a concrete and cement menagerie of life-size animals – giraffe, panda, elephant, stags – interspersed with heroes and neighbours; Lawrence of Arabia rides a camel in this garden in Northumberland. A fifty-first birthday party Charles Burnett III gave in Hampshire in June 2007 (as reported in the *Daily Telegraph*) involved hiring twenty off-duty soldiers to re-enact skirmishes from the Falklands War, with mock bombs to be dropped from swooping Harvard fighter planes in front of his party guests. For such reasons was the Noise Abatement Act passed into the statute books in 1960.

Gardens are for building in, too; spare money and time has resulted in a country packed with edificial gestures. The word folly could have been invented for a column erected by Lord McAlpine in his Hampshire garden in reaction to the government abandoning a wealth tax in 1976. On it are inscribed the words '*Hoc monumentum magno pretio quod aliter in manus publicanorum quandoque cedisset aedificatum*' (This monument was built with a large sum of money that would otherwise have gone to the Inland Revenue). Designed by Quinlan Terry, this was to please himself and amuse his friends – exactly the same reason grottoes, temples and hermitages were dotted around gardens in earlier periods. A poem of 1763 mocked the bourgeois 'cit' for his rococo garden house:

> The trav'ler with amazement sees
> A temple, Gothic or Chinese,
> With many a bell and tawdry rag on
> And crested with a sprawling dragon.

Also in the eighteenth century both the antiquarian John Britton and the Earl of Pembroke preferred to have their personal Stonehenges, the first in his London garden in St Pancras, the second on a rather grander scale on his estate at Wilton in Wiltshire, not that far from the original.

Do we become nicer human beings under the influence of being in the garden?

That was the view of John Sedding, who retired to West Wickham in Kent at the very end of his life as a leading architect, and published the following the year he died:

> Apart from its other uses, there is no spot like a garden for cultivating the kindly social virtues. Its perfectness puts people upon their best behaviour. Its nice refinement secures the mood for politeness . . . Here if anywhere will the human hedgehog unroll himself and deign to be companionable. Here friend Smith, caught by its nameless charm, will drop his brassy gabble and deign to be idealistic; and Jones, forgetful of the main chance of 'bulls' and 'bears' will throw the rein to his sweeter self, and reveal that latent elevation of soul and tendency to romance known only to his wife.

George Llewellyn Davis 'within four paces of a tiger'
(J.M. Barrie's dog in a tiger mask)
at Black Lake in 1901.

The same terrain can, of course, present different ideas to different individuals, as illustrated by the attitudes of J.M. Barrie and his actress wife Mary Ansell to their garden of Black Lake Cottage near Farnham in Surrey. In the August of 1901 Barrie spent days in the garden with the sons of his friends Sylvia and Arthur Llewellyn Davis; here he, adopting the character 'Captain Swarthy', choreographed the boys in the enactment of an imaginary world of pirates, ships, islands, lagoons and huts. The pet St Bernard,

Porthos, was given a mask and disguised as a tiger, and the brothers were armed with garden tools and even long-handled knives. Barrie photographed these events and described them with headings such as 'Fearful Hurricane – Wreck of the Anna Pink – we go crazy for want of food – Proposal to eat Peter – Land Ahoy!' A decade later Mary Ansell (by then divorced) described her love for that place in her book *The Happy Garden*. Whereas Barrie had transformed the lake into the South Seas, for Mary it was simply a place where she watched the herons and the moon reflected in the water. She waxes gushingly lyrical about her hexagonal tea house with its green deck chairs and cushions, a place of 'sweet dreams'.

J.M. Barrie captioned this photograph 'We strung him up' in his record of the summer of 1901, which he printed privately and entitled 'The Boy Castaways of Black Lake Island'.

However, there is a sense that she had not been married to Barrie for nothing: 'In summer nights the tea-house and the bridge are hung with Japanese lanterns, and then the spirit of youth comes down, and there is an end to being grown up, and the most hardened Londoner becomes a child.' Nor is it surprising to find the erstwhile wife of the man who invented Tinkerbell writing that circular formations of funghi under her pine trees could be a place for the 'wood people' to dance around. She notes the 'mossy cushions' and finds it hard to relinquish the fantasy that this is where they have had a parliament, an eisteddfod or a Revivalist meeting.

That such whimsical fairy fantasy belongs in the garden two young Yorkshire girls from Cottingley, Elsie Wright and Frances Griffiths, shrewdly knew

Mary Ansell's Japanese-style tea house: frontispiece illustration by Charles Dawson to her book about Black Lake Cottage, *The Happy Garden*, 1912.

when they concocted the elfin photographs that so excited Conan Doyle in 1917. Rose Fyleman embedded the notion that 'There are fairies at the bottom of our garden! . . ./ You pass the gardener's shed . . .' in her 1920s poem for children; and it appears that the odd twenty-first-century adult still half wishes to cleave to the concept: for sale on the Internet, for as little as £9, there is a choice of miniature model fairy doorways that, when placed on a tree or wall in the garden, will 'let the fairies in'.

A more universal experience of the garden is sheer delight in it. In a letter of 4 July 1739, Alexander Pope wrote of Stowe, one of the grandest gardens in Georgian England, 'I am every hour in it, but dinner and night, and every hour envying myself the delight of it.' For Francis Kilvert, 'sitting under the shade of the acacia on the lawn' in an ordinary Victorian garden in Wales on 23 September 1873, 'enjoying the still warm sunshine of the holy autumn day it was a positive luxury to be alive.' Their words remind us that, whatever we choose to do in our private Edens, the garden is essentially a place for pleasure.

A back garden in wartime, photographed for *Picture Post* magazine in summer 1942 for a story entitled 'How to Spend a Holiday in London'.

1 A PLACE OF ESCAPE AND INSPIRATION

The fact that the British have always preferred living in detached houses and terraces, rather than apartments, has meant that a remarkably large proportion of the population have had access to a garden, however large or small. To step out of the house and into the garden is the quickest way to find solitude and escape. Within the garden cabins, huts, hermitages and numerous other small edifices offer further insulation from the world.

ESCAPE FROM STRESS

In 1618 William Lawson, a Yorkshire clergyman, wrote a treatise on how to grow fruit, *A New Orchard & Garden*, in which he expresses the firm opinion that there is no better place than the garden to recover equilibrium. Addressing himself to overworked lawyers, merchants and politicians – 'the gods of the earth' – he suggests that they should withdraw from their hectic life with 'troublesome affayres of their estate, being tired with the hearing and judging of litigious Controversies, choaken (as it were) with the close aire of their sumptuous Buildings, their stomachs cloyed with variety of Banquets, their ears filled and over-burthened with tedious discoursings' and repair to their gardens and orchards. This idea clearly struck a chord and Gervase Markham repeated the piece in *A Way to Get Wealth*, which stayed in print until the end of the century. Lawson, whose book overflows with his enthusiasm, declared that a garden 'makes all our senses swimme in pleasure' and recommends that it should have 'large walks, broad and long, close and open, like the Tempe groves in Thessalie, raysed with gravell and sand, having seats and banks of Camamile, all this delights the mind, and brings health to the body.'

'God the first garden made, and the first city Cain' is the most famous line written by the seventeenth-century poet and gardener Abraham Cowley. He had experienced life as a courtier, and in his poem 'The Garden' expresses a deep longing to escape:

O blessed shades! O gentle cool retreat
From all th'immoderate heat,
In which the frantic world does burn and sweat!

In the poem he acknowledges the Greek philosopher Epicurus (342–270 BC), who believed that a healthy body and a tranquil soul could be achieved by withdrawal into the garden – albeit on a permanent basis, rather than a temporary one. 'You must free yourself from the prison of politics and the daily round,' Epicurus taught Greeks in his Athens garden. The passionate gardener Sir William Temple applauded the philosopher's way of life, writing in an essay, 'Upon the Gardens of Epicurus; or, of Gardening in the Year 1685', 'The sweetness of the air, the pleasantness of the smells, the verdure of plants, the cleanness and lightness of foods, the exercises of working and walking; but above all, the exemption from cares and solicitude, seem equally to favour and improve both contemplation and health, the enjoyment of sense and imagination, and thereby the quiet and ease of both the body and mind.' Since Temple spent many years as envoy to Brussels and the Hague, and was called out of retirement to negotiate a treaty with the Dutch, he knew the need for a sense of release all too well.

Three hundred and fifty-one years after William Lawson, garden designer John Brookes echoed his words almost exactly: 'As working life becomes more and more hectic and communal pleasures more varied, it seems more than ever essential that the individual and his family should have some place into which they can retreat; somewhere quiet where they have time to think, and can enjoy and refresh themselves by re-establishing contact with nature.' This was the introduction of *Room Outside*, which was groundbreaking in that it not only looked at how a garden should be planted but also planned for what might happen in it.

FOR INSPIRATION

Thinking as you pace up and down the garden has always had devotees and often influenced the shape of the owner's garden. The Elizabethan Francis Bacon, a politician and writer, liked to think and dictate at Gorhambury, as John Aubrey describes in *Brief Lives*: 'a dore opens into a place as big as an ordinary park, the west part whereof is Coppice-wood, where are Walkes cut-out as straight as in a line, and broad enough for a coach, a quarter of a mile long or better. Here his Lordship much meditated, his servant Mr. Bushell attending him with his pen and inke horne to sett down his present Notions.' A couple of centuries later Charles Darwin worked out his scientific theories as he paced around his Sandwalk at Down House in Kent. In his *Reminiscences* (1887) his son Francies wrote: 'The Sand-walk was planted by my father with a variety of trees, such as hazel, alder, lime, hornbeam, birch, privet and dogwood, and with a long line of hollies all down the exposed side. In earlier times he took a certain number of turns every day, and used to count them by means of a heap of flints, one of which he kicked out on the path each time he passed.'

For those who do not favour thinking on their feet, and who don't have a Thomas Bushell following with pen and ink, there has always been the option of creating a spot specifically intended for thinking (although Isaac Newton was reputedly simply drinking tea in the garden after dinner at Woolsthorpe Manor in Lincolnshire when it occurred to him to wonder why the apple falling off the tree fell down, rather than upwards or sideways). Mounts or raised walks were common features in sixteenth- and seventeenth-century gardens; these were occasionally grandly named Mount Parnassus after the home of Apollo and the nine Muses, thus giving a broad hint that they were intended for inspiration. Anne of Denmark had a Mount Parnassus at Somerset House in the Strand, as did Prince Henry at Richmond Palace.

The Georgians, too, considered suitably equipped spots for aspiring thinkers and poets to be interesting garden features. Writer and garden designer Stephen Switzer describes a tempting example at Dyrham in Gloucestershire in *The Nobleman, Gentleman, and Gardener's Recreation*: a 'seat round an aspiring Fir-tree in the Centre . . . I never in my whole life did see so agreeable a Place for the sublimest Studies as this in the Summer, and here are small Desks erected in Seats for that Purpose.' Frances Seymour, Countess of Hartford, evokes a similar atmosphere in a letter dated May 1740, to her friend Henrietta Louisa, Countess of Pomfret, in which she describes her garden, Richings in Buckinghamshire: 'There is one walk I am extremely partial to; which is rightly called the Abbey-walk, since it is composed of prodigiously high beech trees, that form an arch through the whole length, exactly resembling a cloister. At one end is a statue; and about the middle a tolerably large circle, with Windsor chairs round it: and I think, for a person of contemplative disposition, one would scarcely find a more venerable shade in any poetic description.'

When William Wordsworth set up home with his sister Dorothy at Dove Cottage in the Lake District on a shoestring – they papered the cottage with newspaper – and set out to make a life dedicated to poetry, their romantic inspiration was in nature. Dorothy records in her journal the sitting places in their garden that she devised with their friend Samuel Taylor Coleridge to enable William to write outside. '1 October 1800: After dinner Coleridge discovered a rock-seat in the orchard. Cleared away the brambles. Coleridge obliged to go to bed after tea . . . I broiled Coleridge a mutton chop which he ate in bed.' Two weeks later she records: 'A fine clear morning. After William had composed a little, I persuaded him to go into the orchard. The prospect most divinely beautiful from the seat – all colours melting into each other.'

Henry Percy, 9th Earl of Northumberland, by Nicholas Hilliard, painted lying in a garden in a melancholic and poetic pose, *c*.1595.

Two years later she recounts building a bower in the garden. Saturday, 1 May 1802: 'A heavenly morning. As soon as breakfast was over we went into the garden and sowed the scarlet beans around the house . . . We then went and sate in the orchard till dinner time. It was very hot. William wrote the Celandine. We planned a shed for the sun was too much for us.' On Wednesday: 'A very fine morning rather cooler than yesterday. We planted ¾ ths of the Bower', and on Thursday it was finished: 'A Sweet morning. We have put the finishing stroke to our Bower and here we are sitting in the orchard. It is one o'clock . . . It is a nice cool shady spot. The small Birds are singing. Lambs bleating, Cuckow calling. The Thrush sings by fits. Thomas Ashburner's axe is going quietly (without passion) in the orchard. Hens are cackling, Flies humming, the women talking together at their doors . . .' The weather stays fine and on Saturday Dorothy 'read Henry V in the bower while William lay on his back on the seat.'

A tree-house retreat; detail from an engraving of Pishobury, from Sir Henry Chauncy's *Historical Antiquities of Hertfordshire*, 1700.

WRITING AND THINKING IN THE GARDEN

Practical garden thinkers have generally created something more substantial for all-weather use. The fact that 'all studious and learned men have exceedingly delighted in a solitary and rural habitation, and have much preferred it, for the serenity of the Air, and the pleasing VIRIDITY, which much quickens the Genius' was noted by John Worlidge in his popular book *Systema Horticulturae, or, The Art of Gardening* of 1677, still in print in 1716 as *The Gentleman's Companion, in the business and pleasures of a Country Life*. Solitary retreats were popular in the seventeenth century. A judge, Sir Nicholas Lechmere, built himself a little pavilion in the garden of his house at Severn End, Hanley Castle, near Worcester, where he would spend several days at a time, immersed in his books. His study had a little slit, similar to a leper's squint in a church, through which he could observe his orchards, even if he was not actually sitting in them. During the Civil War John Evelyn, living at his brother's house at Wotton in Surrey and oppressed by the state of the country, turned to gardening and built himself what he called a hermitage: 'a little study over a Cascade, to pass my Melancholy houres shaded there with Trees, & silent Enough'. In *Brief Lives* John Aubrey regretted that Sir John Denham, who lived through the Civil War at his parsonage-house in Egham, 'was wont to say (before the troubles) that he would built a Retiring-place to entertain his muses; but the warres forced him to sell that as well as the rest'.

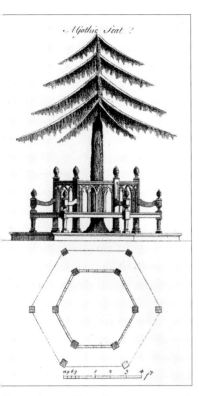

Pattern for a gothic garden seat to surround a fir tree, from Charles Over's *Ornamental Architecture* of 1758.

Poets have, perhaps unsurprisingly, been particularly fond of finding their muse in the garden. In the 1770s William Cowper had the loan of his next-door neighbour's summer house. He called it various things, including his sulking room, but it was also his retreat and 'a refuge from intrusion'. He describes his day in a letter: 'As soon as breakfast is over, I retire to my nutshell of a summer house which is my verse manufactory.' Cowper's pleasure in the place is evident: 'I write in a nook I call my bouderie; it is a Summerhouse not much bigger than a Sedan chair, the door of which opens into the garden that is now crowded with pinks, roses and honeysuckles and the window into my neighbour's orchard.' Towards the end of his life he put up four lines of his own verse on his garden hut, where he spent time with his wife:

> This cabin, Mary, in my sight appears,
> Built as it has been in our waning years,
> A rest afforded to our weary feet
> Preliminary to – the last retreat.

When Wordsworth married and became an established poet, he moved from Dove Cottage to the larger Rydal Mount, and graduated from Dorothy's romantic and natural bowers to a more formal wooden writing hut with an interior lined with patterns of twig mosaic. The hut, which looks much as if it came from a Victorian catalogue, gave him views of Lake Grasmere and the peace from his family and visitors that he still craved. George Bernard Shaw, too, liked to remove himself from the house to write. He appropriated as his study a wooden summer house that his wife Charlotte had ordered for the garden of their new house at Ayot St Lawrence. It was the latest type, revolving on rails so that it could always face the sun. For working in it was small and characteristically spartan, but it had electricity for heat and light, a telephone connection to the house and a bunk for naps. For nearly fifty years Shaw retreated there to work peacefully every day with an alarm clock to tell him when it was lunchtime. His staff could protect him from intrusion by stating honestly that he was out, although Nancy Astor was reported as attempting to burst into his solitude by banging on the door of the hut with the words: 'Come out of there, you old fool. You've written enough nonsense in your life!'

Jane, wife of the historian Thomas Carlyle, was at least as resourceful as Dorothy Wordsworth and lived as Dorothy did with a genius whose condition of life was his *raison d'être*. In the hot summer of 1857 Jane decided to create an awning in their Chelsea garden to enable Thomas to work in shade 'away from the blazes of July'. She sewed sheets together and suspended them from tree branches and poles attached to the garden wall, and then went away on holiday. Carlyle obediently

George Bernard Shaw, photographed looking classically pensive on the step of his writing hut, shortly before his ninetieth birthday.

worked there, correcting the proofs of his life of Frederick the Great. The weather broke and she was not there to encourage him to go indoors. He wrote to Jane on 26 July 1857 complaining, 'I have had for about a week past a fit (villanouse [sic] headaches, feverishness etc) *wh* I at first attributed to *Oxtail soup*, but now discover to be *cold*, caught sitting in the sweep of the wind under that awning: – I have put on my flannel again.' The awning was an improvement on a construction that she had rigged up for herself outside several years earlier using washing line, poles and an old floor cloth when the noise and mess of builders in the house was too much to bear. She sat in an armchair with her sewing and letters and continued her normal chores outside under its shade.

Thomas Carlyle sitting under his awning, as he appeared from the top floor of his house in Chelsea: photograph by Robert Tait.

A PLACE FOR MOODS

The engraved frontispiece of Robert Burton's widely read book *The Anatomy of Melancholy*, first published in 1621, is panelled in sections, each one representing symptoms and attributes of different types of the melancholy condition. In the central position is an image of Democritus of Abdera meditating. He holds the classic melancholy pose, his head leaning on one hand. Behind is a balustrade and below him is a classic seventeenth-century walled garden with corner gazebo. Shady bowers and suggestive darkness were the scenery required to elicit a worthwhile burst of melancholy.

The garden pictured here is

in a form that would have been familiar to John Donne, whose lovesick protagonist in his early seventeenth-century poem 'Twicknam Garden' cries as he enters the garden:

> Blasted with sighs,
> and surrounded with teares.
> Hither I come to seeke the spring,

and exclaims:

> Make me a mandrake,
> so I may grow here,
> Or a stone fountaine weeping out
> my yeare.

Detail from the frontispiece of Robert Burton's *The Anatomy of Melancholy*. Democritus sits under the shade of a tree on rough turf.

A poetic or contemplative mood might be prompted by the use of mottoes. The unsurpassed master of this form was a poet himself, named William Shenstone, who created The Leasowes in Warwickshire, one of the most visited gardens of the mid-eighteenth century. He devised a route round his five acres on which he placed more than thirty benches, most of which were accompanied by a quotation or inscription — some merely signs painted on wood. Each one invited a particular thought from the visitor. For one in a 'retired situation' he chose a quotation from Horace (*Me gelidum nemus/ Nympharumque lelves cum satyris chori/Secernant populo*), helpfully translated in a guide to the garden published by Robert Dodsley as

> May the cool grove,
> And gay assembled nymphs with sylvans mix'd
> Conceal me from the world!

Shenstone paid homage to the most celebrated poet of the age, Alexander Pope, with a quotation from *Eloisa to Abelard*, which suggested that a certain view offered 'Divine Oblivion of low-thoughted Care'. He also created memorial seats for meditating on friends or heroes. One thanked the poet James Thomson, best remembered for 'Rule Britannia', who had died in 1748 just as Shenstone was starting his garden, for his muse and two further seats commemorated the friendship and the merits of Shenstone's lifelong Oxford friends Richard Jago and Richard Graves, both poets as well as clerics.

The idea of the garden being a suitable place for remembrance was gaining in popularity at that time. Pope had put up a memorial to his mother Edith, which he surrounded with evergreen cypresses – classical symbols of immortality; and Jean-Jacques Rousseau's tomb on an island in a lake at the landscape garden at Ermenonville, where he ended his days, was one of the most famous sites in Europe. The idea persisted, even if just reduced to an ornamental garden feature in that part of the garden 'exclusively devoted to solitude and meditation', and was proposed as a project by the Regency architect J.B. Papworth in *Hints on Ornamental Gardening*.

'Superior gardens are composed of glooms and solitudes, not of plants and trees' was the belief of the Scottish poet, artist and gardener Ian Hamilton Finlay, whose garden Little Sparta in Lanarkshire, begun in 1966, returned to the idea of using a garden to prompt thought and discourse by carefully placing words and poems carved in stone within a landscape.

A bit of solitude leads to introspection, and a garden is the perfect place to indulge in teenage moods or misery. As a fifteen-year-old, the novelist Fanny Burney certainly saw the garden as a place for melancholy. She confided to her diary in 1768 while on a visit to her stepmother's house adjoining the churchyard at Lynn Regis in Norfolk: 'It is a sweet, mild evening, I will take a turn in the garden . . . [it] is very small, but very, very prettily laid out – the greatest part is quite a grove, and three people might be wholly concealed from each other with ease in it. I scarce ever walk in it, without becoming grave, for it has the most private, lonely shady, *melancholy* look in the world.' Maybe the mood was partly engendered by the boredom of quiet country life, dramatically different from her London existence with her father in

Poland Street, with a constant stream of visitors and outings to concerts, opera and theatre. But Fanny is enchanted with the little gazebo at the end of the garden with a view of the water and describes it as a 'cabin' – a word used to describe a small hideaway and full of connotations. In Fanny's case it means a place in which to write down her intimate feelings. She writes, 'I always spend the evening, sometimes all the afternoon, in this sweet Cabin – except sometimes, when unusually thoughtful, I prefer the garden . . . I cannot express the pleasure I have in writing down my thoughts, at the very moment – my opinion of people when I first see them, and how I alter, or how confirm myself in it – . . .' and confesses to her diary: 'I am going to tell you something concerning myself, which, (if I have not chanced to mention it before) will, I believe, a little surprise you – it is, that I scarce wish for anything so truly, really, and very greatly, as to be *in love*.'

Extreme emotion was the stuff of the drama-soaked novel written by the eccentric and exceptionally wealthy collector William Beckford under the pseudonym Rt. Hon. Lady Harriet Marlowe: *Modern Writing or The Elegant Enthusiast; and Interesting Emotions of Arabella Bloomville* (1796). Being moody in the garden is one of the few realistic moves that Arabella makes ('seventeen summers only had bleached her snowy bosom, yet the fatal experience of evil had more than doubled her years'). The garden of her elegant and retired cottage is appropriately dramatic with 'sapphire rivulet . . . a majestic grove of aged oaks nodded in awful and sublime splendour on one side, while abrupt and fantastic rocks added dignity to the scene on the other'; she indulges her tender grief and sits for hours with her blushing cheek pressed upon her lily hand. Later reflecting on the 'capricious instability' of her lover, the six-foot-two Henry Lambert ('grecian nose, sparkling hazel eyes . . . most beautiful mouth and teeth ever beheld . . . alabaster complexion'), she sits by moonlight on a favourite green bench on the margin of a bubbling stream, 'reading her beloved Ariosto and eating golden pippins, while tears would incessantly chase one another down her innocent nose'.

Mrs Gaskell's seventeen-year-old heroine Molly Gibson in *Wives and Daughters* (1866) rushes headlong to a deserted walk in the garden after her father announces that he is remarrying.

When she had once got to the seat, she broke out with suppressed passion of grief. She did not care to analyse the source of her tears and sobs – her father was going to be married again – her father was angry with her; she had done very wrong – he had gone away displeased; she had lost his love; he was going to be married – away from her – away from his child – his little daughter – forgetting her own dear, dear mother. So she thought in a tumultuous kind of way, sobbing till she was wearied out, and had to gain strength by being quiet for a time, to break forth into her passion of tears afresh. She had cast herself on the ground – that natural throne for violent sorrow – and leant up against the old moss-grown seat; sometimes burying her face in her hands; sometimes clasping them together, as if by the tight painful grasp of her fingers she could deaden mental suffering.

GARDEN BUILDINGS FOR ATMOSPHERE

Grottoes and hermitages in time became whimsical conceits in fashionable gardens. However, it is possible to imagine that many of the original builders saw them as prompts for atmosphere – awestruck and sombre in dark rocky grottoes or spiritually contemplative in hermitages. William Beckford was also an inveterate builder, at Fonthill, his estate in Wiltshire; he had both a hermit's cave and a grotto. In *Arabella Bloomville* he imagines the ultimately excessive grotto, belonging to Lord Mahogany, which maybe hints at his aspiration. To reach it you descended through the shrubbery, down into a forest with deep recesses and mournful cypress trees, and along numerous intricate paths that took you to the entrance of a spacious cave – 'All here was hushed and silent . . . round this cave no gaudy flowers were permitted to bloom; this spot was sacred to pale lilies and violets' – and opened out to an immense rocky amphitheatre, part of which was a bath 'ornamented with branches of coral, brilliant spars and curious shells. A lucid spring filled a marble bason in the centre, and then losing itself for a moment underground, came dashing and sparkling forth at the extremity of the

cave and took its course over some shining pebbles to the lake below . . .
Here stretched supinely on a bed of moss, the late Lord Mahogany would
frequently pass the sultry hours of day.' Lord Charles Oakley, the subsequent
owner, added the heady scent of tuberose, jessamine and orange trees
planted in tubs and 'Here all his thoughts were engrossed by the subject
of his flame. Here he formed schemes of delusive joys, stifled the rising

sigh, stopped the flowing tear, and
in social converse with his dear
friend Henry Lambert would
oftentimes smoke a comfortable
pipe, when the soft radiance of
the moon played upon the pearly
bosom of the adjacent waters.'

William Beckford's 'rhap-
sodical romance', as he called it, is
a far cry from a grotto built in the
1630s by Thomas Bushell at
Enstone in Oxfordshire. A
speculator and mining engineer,
it was he who had also been Sir
Francis Bacon's amanuensis and
he was, according to John Aubrey,
'the greatest master of the art of
running in Debt (perhaps) in the
world'. No doubt the garden at
Enstone contributed. He was
inspired by a limestone stream,
which calcified, producing

The exterior of Thomas Bushell's grotto at
Enstone underneath his hermitage with its gothic
windows, and set behind a water spout.

curiously shaped stones – perfect grotto-building material: 'The workman
had not worked an hower before he discovers not only a Rock, but a rock
of unusuall figure with Pendants like Icecles as at Wokey Hole, Somerset,
which was the occasion of making that delicate Grotto.' The hillside faced
south, making it a sunny place 'to sitt and read, or contemplate'. In addition,
a water spout played at the mouth of the grotto, creating an artificial

rainbow whenever the sun shone. 'He did not encumber him selfe with his wife, but here enjoyed himself thus in this Paradise till the War brake out.' He entertained Charles I here in 1635 and the following year, with amusements such as a fountain that kept a silver ball in the air and a speechifying hermit. Robert Plot in *The Natural History of Oxfordshire* (1677) describes how over the 'divers Pipes between the Rocks' a banqueting house had been built and 'several other small Closets for divers uses', so it is no wonder that during the Civil War 'his Hermitage over the Rocks at Enston were hung with black-bayes'. The king and his courtiers were long gone by the time John Evelyn visited Enstone in the October of 1664 and described it as a place of 'extraordinary solitude'. He found Bushell, who 'lay in a hamoc like an Indian' among the Egyptian mummies in the grotto, thus living up to his sobriquet the Enstone Hermit.

erior of the grotto at Enstone. Both this and the illustration osite are engravings from *The Natural History of Oxfordshire* by Robert Plot, 1677.

In contrast, it is difficult to imagine Lord Shaftesbury at Wimborne St Giles doing anything with his off-the-peg grotto other than showing it off to visitors. It is described by one traveller: 'There is also a most beautiful grotto finished by Mr. Castles of Marybone; it consists of a winding walk and an anti-room. These are mostly made of rock spar, &c., adorn'd with moss. In the inner room is a great profusion of the most beautiful shells, petrifications, and fine polished pebbles, and there is a chimney to it which is shut up with doors covered with shells, in such a manner as that it does not appear.' Mrs Delany, an artist with a passionate enthusiasm for gardens

Pen-and-ink drawing of William Stukeley's hermitage
at Stamford, 1738.

and plants, and indefatigable garden visitor and a busy correspondent makes frequent reference to grottoes planned and under way.

The idea of a hermitage was equally appealing, although contemporary accounts suggest that maybe serious and solitary contemplation was not always their sole purpose. Hermitage construction could also involve a different sort of scavenging. The antiquarian William Stukeley made a drawing of the one he built in his garden in Stamford in Lincolnshire, a hotch-potch of architectural salvage from local churches in the process of demolition and restoration. Oddly, the cupola, complete with bell that he rang each morning ('a most agreeable exercise'), which sounded suitable for a hermitage was actually added to his wife's Temple of Flora, where she stored her pot plants.

Mrs Delany describes a visit to Lord Orrery's in Ireland in a letter to her sister on 2 August 1748. Beginning 'he is very well-bred and entertaining . . . she delights in *farming*, and he in *building and gardening*, and he has very good taste', she goes on to say that they are in the process of building a new house, though nothing is completed yet but an *hermitage*, which is about an acre of ground – an island, planted with all the variety of trees, shrubs, and flowers that will grow in this country, abundance of little winding walks, differently embellished with little seats and banks; in the midst is placed an hermit's cell, made of the roots of trees, the floor is paved with pebbles, there is a couch made of matting, and little wooden stools, a table with a manuscript on it, a pair of spectacles, a leathern bottle; and hung up in different parts, an hourglass, a weatherglass and several mathematical instruments, a shelf of books, another of wooden platters and bowls, another of earthenware ones, in short everything that you might imagine necessary for a recluse.

Lord Orrery also had an equally theatrical hermitage at his English estate at Marston House in Somerset, which a travelling Irish cleric named Richard Pococke saw in July 1754 and described in his journal: 'At the other end of the garden in a corner is a little Hermitage near finished for my Lord's youngest son; there is a deep way cut down to it with wood on each side, a seat or two in it – one is made in the hollow of a tree; it leads to a little irregular court, with a fence of horses'heads and bones. It is a cabin, poorly thatch'd, and a bedstead covered with straw at one end, a chimney at the other, and some beginning made of very poor furniture.' Which sounds suitably gloomy.

At the same time Lady Luxborough, an obsessive gardener who had acquired everything fashionable for the garden of her house, called Barrells (to which her estranged husband had exiled her), wrote to her friend and neighbour William Shenstone, 'A Mr. Gough of Perry-Hall was here, about three weeks ago, to ask leave to see my Hermitage, and said he liked it. I do not enjoy it much myself: the cold weather and incessant rain would hinder me, were I even in better spirits. Indeed you will say, it is just a proper place for indulging melancholy thoughts; which is true; but therefore I ought to shun it.' This was written towards the end of her life.

For those without the imagination of Thomas Bushell or William Beckford, such buildings were easily found in pattern books. William Wrighte, for example, produced a collection of plans entitled *Grotesque*

Architecture, or Rural Amusement, which included a 'Hermit's Cell with Rustic Seat Attach'd'. His 'Winter Hermitage', made of flints and rough stone and 'lined with wool or any other warm substance intermixed with moss', is in fact, he suggests, a shelter from hunting and wild-fowling, so it was a hermitage in name only. Usually the intention in building a hermitage was to create the effect of somewhere uncomfortably rocky, a remote wilderness if not worthy of St Jerome at least suitable for someone to be persuaded or paid to lurk in during the summer months when the garden was on show, as Gilbert White's brother Harry did when visitors came to look round the garden at Selborne in Hampshire.

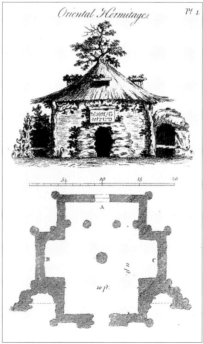

Patterns for hermitages by William Wrighte, published in 1767;
his book *Grotesque Architcture* also included designs
for huts and cascades.

Engraving from the title page of the 1813 edition of *The Natural History of Selborne* by Gilbert White: the hermit surveying the Hampshire countryside from 'his straw-clad cell'.

The tendency to create private garden zones in which to retreat is one that endures. It seems to be primarily masculine, the implication of that being that while the house is the woman's domain, parts of the garden can be the man's. In the eighteenth century the Duke of Newcastle threw dice and gambled at hazard in his belvedere at Claremont in Surrey, while Sir Francis Dashwood indulged in his passion for cockfighting in a secluded room above a classic Tuscan archway at West Wycombe. *Kind Hearts and Coronets*, the 1950 Ealing film comedy, memorably has Alec Guinness, as Henry d'Ascoyne, repeatedly retiring to his garden shed, ostensibly to develop photographs but also to drink behind the back of his fiercely teetotal wife, Edith. The garden retreat is where hobbies and interests can be pursued uninterrupted and undisturbed.

A 'precious antithesis to the home' is what Tom Fort calls the shed, writing on the subject of English men and lawn-mowing in *The Grass is Greener* (2000).

> It speaks to him of an older, more elemental life. It is a place where he is master, where standards other than those of cleanliness and neatness and newness apply. To our man, the harsh monosyllable – 'shed' – has a comforting, spiritual resonance. His secular self acknowledges that it is a dumping ground for tools, machinery, teetering towers of old flowerpots, cobweb-festooned stacks of garden chairs with rotted

canvas seats, bags of Growmore, packets of ant powder, bottles of weedkiller with tops that will not turn, brushes rigid with ancient creosote, drums of unruly wire netting with last autumn's leaves held crispy in the mesh, loops of wire hanging from rusty nails, saws with rusting teeth which he has intended to oil and clean these past five years, and a great accumulation of other relics.

But to him it is much more than a mere storage space. It is a sanctum, a private place where his soul is nourished. It should have the quiet of a chapel, although in a good cause it may be fractured by electric drill or thumping hammer blows. There is much dust, but it lies still, and the old flies caught in the cobwebs in the corners are undisturbed. The shed is like his mind, crammed with the forgotten, the half-forgotten and the redundant. It is a place to pause, to contemplate, to sniff that rich, musty, old smell, to pick up things and put them down again, to arrange and rearrange.

For many families during the Second World War the garden became a literal place of escape with the creation of air-raid shelters. The instructions for building one involved digging a hole 7 feet 6 inches long and 6 feet wide to a depth of 4 feet and bolting together sections of protective corrugated steel, which had to then be covered with at least 15 inches of soil. Most shelters had earth floors and people generally found them oppressively cold, damp and dark. In an unpublished memoir of wartime Birmingham, Gwendolen Watts remembers her family's Andersen shelter, built by her father, who had

> dug a huge crater in the garden . . . He had put steps there that went round and round so if there was a bomb blast it would stop it coming straight into the entrance. He painted the inside of the shelter white and he'd got butterflies painted on the walls. He had a little stove down there, it was a real home from home. He put bunk beds on each side for us because he was always out fire watching. As soon as we'd had our meal we'd go down there with our books and our knitting, whatever we were doing.

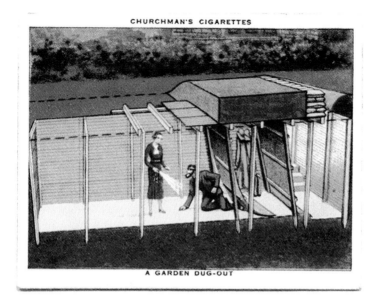

CHURCHMAN'S CIGARETTES

A GARDEN DUG-OUT

'Planning a Refuge', one of a series of forty-eight cigarette cards on
Air Raid Precautions published in 1938.

2 A PLACE FOR FRESH AIR AND EXERCISE

Fresh air and exercise is an old mantra for health and happiness and going out in the open air is just a matter of opening the door into a country or suburban garden. However, in the sixteenth and seventeenth centuries frequent recurrence of plague led to a terror of miasmas and bad air, held as the source of disease. The Tudor physician Andrew Boorde chillingly in one of the earliest books in English on what might be called put it preventative medicine, *A Compendyous Regyment or a Dyetary of Helth*, published in 1542: 'There is nothing, except poison, that doth corrupt the blood of man, as doth corrupt and contagious air . . . evil and corrupt airs doth infect the blood, and doth engender many corrupt humours, and doth putrify the brain, and doth corrupt the heart; and therefore it doth breed many diseases and infirmities through the which, man's life is abbreviated and shortened.' One of the solutions to this alarming problem was, he said, to 'plant a fair garden replete with herbs of aromatic and redolent savours'. This was practical, in that it might provide not only an antiseptic area but also a ready supply of nosegay material to gather as you left the house, since having 'some things of sweet savour' in your hands was a way to avoid infection.

A SOURCE OF GOOD HEALTH

Cardinal Wolsey's garden at Hampton Court was his healthy retreat from York Place in London and was so described by his biographer George Cavendish in a poem:

> My gardens sweet, enclosed with walles strong,
> Embanked with benches to sytt and take my rest;
> The knots so enknotted, it cannot be exprest,

With arbours and alyes so pleasant and so dulce,
The pestilent ayaer with flavours to repulse.

Wolsey had recommended Andrew Boorde as a doctor to Henry VIII; it seems, though, from portraits that Wolsey did not take his advice and he died before Boorde's book was published.

Boorde's message is clear:

> After you have evacuated your body and trussed your points, comb your head oft; and so do divers times in the day. And wash your hands and wrists, your face and eyes, and your teeth, with cold water. And after you be apparelled, walk in your garden or park a thousand pace or two . . . before you go to your refection, moderately exercise your body with some labour, or playing at the tennis, or casting a bowl, or poising some weights or plummets of lead in your hands, or some other thing, to open your pores, and to augment natural heat.

In addition he gives advice on healthy situations for house building and on sanitation, and he has thoughts on the garden: 'And among other things, a pair of butts is a decent thing about a mansion; and other while, for a great man, necessary, it is to pass his time with bowls in an alley' for 'when a man hath exercised himself in the daytime, as is rehearsed, he may sleep soundly and surely in God'. In a *Treatise against Diceing and Dancing* of the same period, John Northbroke too recommended that young men should 'labour with poises of lead or other metal'.

GARDENING AS EXERCISE

Unusually for the early eighteenth century, when employing gardeners was a given, John Laurence, Rector of Yelvertoft in Northamptonshire, proselytized in favour of doing the work yourself. In *The Clergyman's Recreation* he enthuses about the benefits of gardening for healthy exercise and relaxation because 'a clergy man whose chief and most constant business is sitting at his study' needed to preserve his health, and unfortunately most sports and exercises were too undignified for a divine. Wresting one's garden from the hands of professional gardeners, for whom he seems to have the utmost contempt, and getting down to some digging was the 'perfect physick' but only 'ad ruborem', not 'ad sudorem' – that is, to achieve an ascetic rosy glow, not a manly sweat. Planting fruit trees and digging paths were his specialities, in particular grass and gravel walks, which offered considerable pleasure to thoughtful and contemplative people. Laurence also emphasizes that writing the book had not led him to neglect his parish duties.

This discussion of grass paths is an early mention of the link between exercise and mowing. Whether or not Laurence's fellow cleric Dean Delany mowed for exercise is not known – his wife mentions him in a letter of 16 June 1750, saying 'he is at this moment up to his chin in haymaking in the lawn under my closet-window, and the whole house is fragrant with the smell of it' – but one imagines he was the sort of man Edwin Budding had in mind when he invented the lawn mower and attached the following sentence to the specification on his 1830 patent: 'Country gentlemen may find in using my machine themselves an amusing, useful and healthy exercise.'

CONCRETE CRAZY PAVING

A CONCRETE EDGE TO THE FLOWER BORDER

Two projects on the 'Garden Hints' card series of 1938 from Wills' cigarettes, both involving concrete.

Now it seems that subjugating grass into neat stripes of darker and lighter green has transcended labour and become a science or healthy sport. This aspect of mowing remains a selling point: a recent review of a very small electric rotary mower was headed 'Keep Fit and Have Lush Lawns' and insisted that biceps could be improved by bracing the legs and swinging the mower from side to side.

Keeping men healthily occupied was the philosophy behind many garden schemes. John Laurence's path digging was an early example of what the Victorians might have called a pastime, which then became a hobby and finally, in the mid-twentieth century, a Do It Yourself project. An 1880 edition of the *Boy's Own Paper* reckoned that making rustic garden

Churchill building a brick wall at Chartwell in 1928, in this case helped by his daughter Sarah.

furniture incorporating 'grotesque growths of clusters of branches' was useful employment for a spare hour, and that 'there is no reason why boys of fair average intelligence should not become expert in this really useful and ornamental work'. In the 1920s and 1930s ready-mix cement and concrete offered men the chance to expend much energy in the creation of all manner of crazy paving and rockeries and in the digging of sunken gardens and ponds.

When Winston Churchill built a wall round his vegetable garden at Chartwell in Kent, paying the gardener's daughter 6d. to pass him bricks, he was doing much the same as what Sid G. Hedges intended his readers to do when in *The Universal Book of Hobbies*, published in the 1920s, he offered them a plan for a double-face rockery wall. Hedges writes in the introduction: 'Is it too much to hope that the various Whitehall Ministries of War may one sane day be replaced by constructive Ministries of the People's Leisure?' Instructions came from all quarters: a 1938 series of cigarette cards with the slightly misleading title 'Garden Hints' ('We know not everything in the garden is flowers. Most of it is hard work and this is a set dedicated to all the things which go into making the garden a place of wonder') illustrated making a water-lily pool and laying a paved surround for the garden seat or a concrete edge to the flower border. By the 1950s brightly coloured magazines such as *Homemaker: the Practical How-to-do-it*

Monthly were offering any number of such garden improvement projects to tempt men outside and throw off the fustiness of a sedentary week in the office.

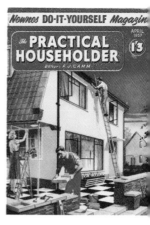

A PLACE TO WALK

Gardens have always been designed as places in which to take the air and walk, whether by tracing patterns in parterres and mazes, strolling on terraces, determinedly striding down vistas or meandering through shrubberies. The gravel walk was of long-standing popularity for the daily ritual of walking in the garden, especially for women who preferred not to trail expensive dress fabrics in mud. In his diary for 22 July 1666 Samuel Pepys recounts a conversation with the architect Hugh May, 'a very

In April 1957 *The Practical Householder* gave instructions for laying a slab path (as well as explaining the byelaws on shed building).

ingenious man', on the current fashion for 'making gardens plain, that we have the best walks of gravell in the world, France having none, nor Italy; and our green of our bowling allies is better than any they have. So our business here being ayre, this is the best way, only with a little mixture of statues, or pots, which may be handsome, and so filled with another pot of such a flower or greene as the season of the year will bear.'

Mrs Delany referred to such constitutional walking as 'terracing'. On 10 October 1737 she described a garden walk in detail in a letter to her mother:

> We came on Saturday as you know, if you are with Sally; the day proved so wet, that I could only take one walk round the garden . . . yesterday the weather was very agreeable – a soft air and no rain; I walked for almost two hours without resting. The trees were so green, and the flowers so sweet, that I was deceived for some time, and *took it for spring*. I walked from one flower-plot to another, till I composed a nosegay of anenomies [sic] carnations, roses, honeysuckles, sweet williams, jessamine, sweet briar, and myrtle, full of pleasing reflections, till unluckily I turned down the lime walk, where the

fluttering of the brown leaves about my ears, and the feuille-mort carpet under my feet, led me back to the latter end of October.

Henrietta Luxborough, although passionate about being in her garden, wrote tartly on the subject in a letter in the spring of 1753: 'I find your neighbours and mine echo each other *Air and Exercise! Air and Exercise!* and we no sooner obey but we get cold, and become incapable of even taking the air which the house and gardens afford. I am sure I find it so; for though I am better in health I have such a violent pain in my face and teeth that I can get not sleep, nor apply myself to anything.'

A young Frenchman, François de la Rochefoucauld, sent on an educational journey by his father to England in 1784, was struck by the peculiar habit of repeatedly walking around one's garden and noted in the observations he wrote for his father: 'Such gentlemen as are not rich enough to have parks have what is called a lawn, a small stretch of land round the house with a number of narrow paths and a little clump of trees, the whole being kept with extreme tidiness. They design these little pleasure-grounds themselves. It is all they need to give them a sense of proprietorship and to provide them with a walk for half an hour before dinner.' At one point during his travels during a particularly rainy and uneventful visit in Norfolk he resorted to building a path for his hosts to relieve his boredom.

Jane Austen was typical of her sex and class in finding walking an essential freedom that allowed women to make visits and run errands independently. Walking and a delight in the fresh air are common themes in her novels. In *Sense and Sensibility* (1811) she describes how the garden is designed for this purpose:

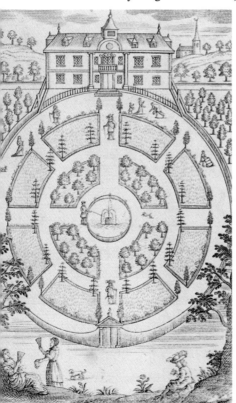

Figures circumnavigate the garden paths in an engraved plate from *Systema Horticulturae; or The Art of Gardening* by John Worlidge, 1688.

'Cleveland was a spacious, modern-built house, situated on a sloping lawn. It had no park, but the pleasure-grounds were tolerably extensive; and like every other place of the same degree of importance, it had its open shrubbery, and closer wood walk; a road of smooth gravel, winding round a plantation, led to the front.' In *Mansfield Park* (1814) when the elderly Mrs Rushworth shows her young visitors round her old-fashioned dark house at Sotherton: 'the young people meeting with an outward door, temptingly open on a flight of steps which led immediately to turf and shrubs, and all the sweets of pleasure-grounds, as by one impulse, one wish for air and liberty, all walked out.' As Regency youth with modern views they find the old-fashioned garden terrace insufferably hot and reject the glare of the bowling green with its iron palisades and turn instead to walk in the up-to-date wilderness 'giving darkness and shade and offering natural beauty . . . They all felt the refreshment of it, and for some time could only walk and admire.' In the same novel, Mrs Grant at the Parsonage, a far smaller property than Sotherton, has a shrubbery for walking in; the patronizing Miss Crawford comments on it: 'it does very well for a place of this sort. One does not think of extent *here* – and between ourselves, till I came to Mansfield, I had not imagined a country parson ever aspired to a shrubbery or anything of the kind.' Fanny Price continues: 'It may seem impertinent in *me* to praise, but I must admire the taste Mrs. Grant has shown in all this. There is such a quiet simplicity in the plan of the walk! not too much attempted!'

Jane Loudon, the hard-working wife of John Claudius Loudon, a garden designer and prolific writer, wrote in 1845 a book called *The Lady's Country Companion; or How to Enjoy a Country Life Rationally*, in the form of letters to a newly married friend explaining the inconveniences of country life but also suggesting ways to enjoy it. She advocated walking in good strong German walking boots that tie around the ankles in order to enjoy wandering through the woods of her own park in the company of a maid, which could be done 'without incurring any very serious dangers . . . You must not suppose, however, that I want you to set forth like a female knight-errant in quest of adventures.'

ARCHERY

The garden as exercise ground was promoted by William Lawson who, in singing the praises of orchards and sharing his fanatical enthusiasm for fruit, points out that they also offered space for physical exertion, in the form of either a bowling alley 'or rather (which is more manly and more healthfull) a payre of Buttes, to stretch your armes'. Lawson was writing in the early seventeenth century, by which time no one was required to defend himself or his country with a bow and arrow. While long hours of archery practice had previously been a compulsory patriotic duty, archery had now become a sport.

The nineteenth-century revival of interest in archery was inspired by the contemporary fascination with all things Gothic and chivalric. Novels, poetry, architecture, painting and furnishings were steeped in the sentiments and style understood to be those of the medieval age. So archery became a popular exercise for Victorian women and allowed them the novelty of being centre stage with the freedom to indulge in something physical. As a sport it required no undignified bending, so the restrictive clothes of the period were not a hindrance, and the equipment was picturesque.

In *The Lady's Country Companion* Jane Loudon opined that archery was a first-class amusement for when unmarried sisters come to stay, since 'few exercises display an elegant form to more advantage.' Was this one way that unmarried sisters might find a husband? Jane Loudon recommends using the old bowling green as an archery site and collecting together a target, proper bows and arrows, bracers, shooting gloves, belt and tassel. The belt, she explains, buckled round the waist and had a pouch for holding arrows, and the tassel was for wiping the arrows clean. However, 'ladies very often omit the belt, as they have generally some person in attendance on them to supply them with arrows, and to pick up and wipe those they have the misfortune to let enter the ground.' If leaving off the belt was a flirtatious ploy, maybe Francis Kilvert, as a young curate in the Welsh Marches, did not realize it. He wrote in his diary in September 1871: 'In the afternoon we went to shoot and play croquet. The Priory people were there, Mrs. Allen, Lucy, Katie, Miss Draper, and lovely little May Oliver with her betwitching face, beautiful dark eyes and golden curls. She was shooting and had no quiver, so I acted as quiver for her, holding her arrows, picking them up, and being her slave generally.' He writes appreciatively of another archery party: 'it was a pretty sight to see the group of ladies with their fresh light dresses moving up and down the long green meadow between the targets, and the arrows flitting and glancing white to and fro against the bank of dark green trees. At 6 tea, coffee, cider cup etc. was laid out in the summer house', but there was bathos on another occasion, when a chicken was killed by someone's arrow.

Shortly after Kilvert wrote this description, William Powell Frith, one of the grandest of Victorian Royal Academicians, must have begun his painting *The Fair Toxophilites*, an almost precise illustration of a scene George Eliot included in her novel *Daniel Deronda* (1876), in which there is an archery meeting, a grand affair taking place at Brackenshaw Park on newly mown turf, the target placed in agreeable afternoon shade: 'What could make a better background for the flower-groups of ladies, moving and bowing and turning their necks as it would become the leisurely lilies to do if they took to locomotion.' The heroine, Gwendolen, is pronounced the finest girl present: 'Who can deny that bows and arrows are among the prettiest weapons in the world for feminine forms to play with? They prompt attitudes full of grace and power, where that fine concentration of energy seen in all marksmanship, is freed from associations of bloodshed . . . has no ugly smell of brimstone, breaks

A highly saleable image: William Powell Frith's painting *The Fair Toxophilites*, painted in 1872 with his two eldest daughters as models.

nobody's shins, breeds no athletic monsters.' As the meeting takes place outside in the garden rather than in a crowded ballroom, men stare at the women with impunity. The women seem to be like racehorses circling the paddock, the onlookers noting their conformation:

> 'That girl is like a high-mettled racer,' said Lord Brackenshaw to young Clintock, one of the invited spectators.
>
> 'First chop! Tremendously pretty too,' said the elegant Grecian, who had been paying her assiduous attention; 'I never saw her look better.'

MECHANICAL HELP

The leading landscape gardener of his age, Humphry Repton had injured his spine in a carriage accident and therefore fully appreciated the needs of the disabled and invalids wishing to take the air in gardens. In his last book, written in 1816, *Fragments on the Theory and Practice of Landscape Gardening*, he proposed that gardens for the wheelchair-bound should have broad verges and glades of mown turf rather than allow them to suffer from 'the grind along a gravel-walk, [when] the shaking and rattling soon

Luxury of Gardens

In *The Luxury of Gardens* Repton illustrates a figure being wheeled beside the raised strawberry beds – the fruit at a convenient level for picking and eating.

become intolerable'. Charmingly, he also advocated raised strawberry beds for those in wheelchairs. John Dawson's 'Bath Chair with Wheels' was invented in 1783; a considerable advance on the cumbersome sedan chair, it made propelling invalids around Bath and other spa towns relatively easy. An illustration in Repton's book shows something very similar. A chair maker in Walham Green called Foulger illustrated an ordinary Windsor chair mounted on a wheeled trolley and something resembling a children's cart on his printed trade card in the 1770s, calling it a 'garden machine'. Lord Percival had described in 1724 how such a chair enabled his wife to see the full extent of the garden at Hall Barn near Beaconsfield: 'the narrow winding walks and paths cut into it are innumerable and a woman in full health cannot walk them all, for which reason my wife was carried in a wheelchair, like those at Versailles, by which means she lost nothing worth seeing'.

Foulger's trade card displays a range of Georgian garden furniture, including a covered seat with a little shelf.

In 1787 James Carmichael Smyth wrote a pamphlet entitled 'An Account of the Effects of Swinging, Employed as a Remedy in the Pulmonary Consumption and Hectic Fever'. The inventor, Joseph Merlin, attempted to capitalize on this theory by inventing the Hygeian chair. On a London visit in 1788 Caroline Lybbe Powys – an energetic Georgian woman who kept a meticulous diary – visited an exhibition of Merlin's various inventions and wrote: 'The portable hygeian chair, by which people may swing themselves with safety, at Merlin's, are very clever, and the physicians say are extremely conducive to health; their motion I found easy and pleasing . . . £40, too expensive for most people merely for pleasure.' It is speculation to think that these chairs might have been taken into the garden, but the characters determinedly swinging in a pleasure garden in Bath, as sketched by John Nixon, look slightly as though they might be doing it for health reasons rather than for the thrill.

SERIOUS EXERCISE

The pursuit of fresh air was part of a late Victorian move towards a healthier life, which also encompassed physical exertion, rational dress and an enthusiasm for the word hygienic. Typical of her age is the heroine of Thomas Hardy's novel *A Laodicean*, Paula Power, who holds 'advanced views on social and other matters' and builds a gymnasium in her garden, fitted out with ropes and bars in imitation of those at the new colleges for women. This hut is kept locked and is hidden in the shrubbery – and no wonder, since Paula dons a pink flannel boy's costume to do her exercises. When Captain de Stancy peeps through a crack in wooden walls he sees an 'optical poem': Paula is 'bending, wheeling and undulating in the air like a gold-fish in its globe . . . "How deuced clever of the girl! She means to live to be a hundred." . . . the white manilla ropes clung about the performer like snakes as she took her exercise, and the colour in her face deepened as she went on.'

Purposeful exercise came under the catch-all phrase of Physical Culture. British soldiers of the Indian Raj had noted the swinging of heavy clubs that Kushti wrestlers used to build up their strength and brought a lighter version home, whereupon Indian clubs became a craze for men, and certain modern young women, at the turn of the century. Explanatory booklets of exercises went on the market; one such was *The Eustace Miles System of Physical Culture* (1907), 'specially compiled for use every evening before retiring, to clear the system and produce a healthy night's rest, at the same time keeping the muscles in the pink of condition' and 'fully illustrated by poses of the Author and a Lady Assistant'. A. Alexander, author of *Healthful Exercises for Girls* (1902), explains that 'The exercises with them are most graceful, and principally intended to develop

John Nixon's observation of the elderly and the weighty on swings, *Bath*, 1800.

the upper part of the body.' Certainly whirling weighted clubs was a garden rather than an indoor activity. Although women did use Indian clubs, the exercise system callisthenics was considered more suitable for females and had a surprisingly long life span. That a young woman was likely to practise callisthenics in the garden is suggested by the appearance they make in the *Girl's Own Book of Amusements*, published in 1876, which states that callisthenic exercises had been recently introduced to England and that many had thought them dangerous 'because they confounded them with the ruder and more daring gymnastics of boys', while they were in fact free from danger and produced vigorous muscles, graceful motion and symmetry of form.

Advertisement for a booklet of teach-yourself Indian Club Exercises, 1907.

Unsurprisingly callisthenics make an appearance in E.F. Benson's sequence of novels set in small town society during the late 1920s and 1930s and featuring two highly competitive women, Miss Elizabeth Mapp and Mrs Emmeline Lucas, known as Lucia (the original character has been ascribed to both Lady Sybil Colefax and Marie Corelli). In *Mapp and Lucia* (1935), Lucia is becoming bored of being in mourning for her husband:

> Like a sensible woman she was very careful of her physical health, and since this stunt of mourning made it impossible for her to play golf or take brisk walks, she sent for a very illuminating little book, called *An Ideal System of Callisthenics for those no longer Young*, and in a secluded glade of her garden she exposed as much of herself as was proper to the invigorating action of the sun, when there was any, and had long bouts of skipping, and kicked, and jerked, and swayed her trunk, gracefully and vigorously, in accordance with the instructions laid down.

Later in the novel the author describes more of her radical behaviour: wearing a dazzling bathing suit of black and yellow, and

> skipping on the little lawn with the utmost vigour . . . Lucia stalked about the lawn with a high prancing motion when she had finished her skipping. Then she skipped again, and then she made some odd jerks, as if she was being electrocuted. She took long deep breaths, she lifted her arms high above her head as if to dive, she lay down on the grass and kicked, she walked on tiptoe like a ballerina, she swung her body round from the hips.

A book sponsored by a rotary mower manufacturer, *The Flymo Book of Garden Games and Lawn Leisure*, published in 1989, offered the following idea, much in the spirit of the late twentieth century, for turning your lawn into a gymnasium. Weight training for both men and women alike with a couple of household bricks would be effective, or

> there is nothing to stop you at least in investing in a keep fit tape so that you can don your personal hi-fi – or put speakers at an open window – and have a daily work-out in the fresh air . . . The only factor that might affect your enthusiasm for the idea is the proximity of your neighbours – unless, that is, you're an exhibitionist by nature! – but then you can always put paid to prying eyes with a few strategically placed ornamental screens.

FRESH COUNTRY AIR

Health and the garden were thus firmly linked, 'Salubrity being one of the advantages expected from a garden,' as John Worlidge writes in his treatise in gardening – a sentiment echoed in poetry in 'The Garden' by his contemporary Abraham Cowley, who famously declared that he wanted nothing as badly as he wanted a small house and a large garden:

> Here health itself does live,
> That salt of life, which does all a relish give
> Its standing pleasure, and intrinsic wealth
> The body's virtue and the soul's good fortune, health.

Contrasting the advantages of life in a city and life in the country is a debate with a long history. In *Systema Horticulturae*, John Worlidge stated that 'country life improves and exercises the most excellent parts of our Intellects'. The wealthy and aristocratic traditionally managed to keep feet firmly in each camp, spending seasons in both. Victorian philanthropists believed that a garden was the best antidote to the evils of urban life, and factory villages such as Bournville, founded by George Cadbury in the

1890s, offered an 'outdoor village life, with opportunities for the natural and healthful occupation of cultivating the soil' in the gardens provided with the cottages.

'Human life, like plant life, flourishes in sun and air and grows pale and anaemic when it is deprived of these,' wrote M.H. Baillie Scott in *Houses and Gardens* (1906) – an appropriate statement for an architect who worked on houses for Letchworth, the first ever garden city. Two years later the German writer on architecture Hermann Muthesius noted the British desire to escape to a country garden: English men and women, he wrote in *Das Englische Haus* (1908), would forgo almost anything, 'theatre, concerts, dinner-parties, the races, at-homes and much else that goes by the name of pleasure for the sake of breathing simple fresh country air and enjoying their gardens and countryside'; offices were increasingly abandoning Saturday morning working and 'already everyone feels that they have the right to leave for the country after work on Friday and return on Monday morning.' The railway companies introduced special weekend tickets. *Country Life*, 'The Journal for all interested in Country Life and Country Pursuits', was founded in 1897 in part to capitalize on this new market for weekend and summer retreats and offered many features on building new manageable country houses. With rural names such as Ridgehanger, Larkcliff, Hilltop, the Cobbles, High Moss, Sunnymead and the Hurst they fulfilled the country dream of the period, their gardens laid out with every amenity – tennis lawn, croquet lawn, rose garden, loggia and summer house – to ensure that maximum use was made of the fresh air.

Simultaneously many families were moving out to newly built suburbs with their winding avenues of semi-detached houses close to the railway or underground line. The front gardens were for display to the road and outside world, but back gardens were for private life. London Underground illustrated such a house on an advertising poster – with tall generous chimney, deep tiled roof with dormer window, the mother winding wool in a deck chair while a child helps at her feet. The husband, his jacket off, waters his bedding plants, and William Cowper's poem 'Sanctuary' is scrolled across the lawn. Ernest Radford expresses the pleasure of escaping from the city in his poem 'Our Suburb', written in 1906:

The suburban idyll: fresh air in Golders Green, promoted
on a London Underground poster, 1908.

He leaned upon the narrow wall
That set the limit to his ground,
And marveled, thinking of it all,
That he such happiness had found.
He had no word for it but bliss;
He smoked his pipe, he thanked his stars;
And what more wonderful than this?
He blessed the groaning stinking cars
That made it doubly sweet to win
The respite of the hours apart
From all the broil and sin and din
Of London's damned money mart.

A PLACE TO SLEEP OUTSIDE

Belief in the advantages of fresh air led to a craze for sleeping out of doors. 'Some of us are getting into the way, anyhow in the dog days, of dragging our beds out under the stars,' contributed H. Avray Tipping in 1911 to a book published by *Country Life* called *The House and its Equipment*. Many new houses built during this period, for example in Hampstead Garden Suburb, were equipped with practical balconies attached to bedrooms, making it easy to pull out a bed on a fine night. Garden huts and summer houses were also pressed into service as temporary outside bedrooms. The authoress Marion Cran describes in her book *The Garden of Ignorance* – written, as she put it, in the 'careless days of peace before 1914' – how she and her guests slept out in her Home Counties garden:

> It is not everyone who has a garden that has a wood; ours has been one of the greatest joys of the cottage. People with nice tidy orderly minds come down for the week-end to rest from the labours of town, and find themselves invited to sleep out in hammocks through the summer nights. They get wrested from the ordinary routine of their days by being taken for long rambles after dinner, and forbidden to dress for that same meal. Towards midnight, when most people

are making for the bedrooms in an orderly and reputable manner, they discover strange shapes flitting about clad in warm dressing-gowns, with blankets thrown over their shoulders, and it ultimately transpires that half the household is bound for the wood, there to spend the summer night in the hammocks.

Nor were babies immune from this enthusiasm. From William Buchan's *Domestic Medicine* of 1769 onwards, childcare manuals encouraged the idea of exposing children to fresh air; it was recommended that they were placed beside a window in small oblong baskets. The subsequent invention of the pram made doing this an easier proposition, as babies no longer had to be carried about in the arms of their mother or nursemaid. Charles Burton patented a design for the perambulator in 1853 and opened a shop in Oxford Street to sell them. During the 1920s faith in fresh air was taken to extremes. *Common Sense in the Nursery* by Charis Frankenburg (1922) together with Marie Stopes' *Your Baby's First Year* (1939) between them saw hardly any need to bring the baby indoors. Mrs Frankenburg opines that 'Infants should hardly be indoors at all between 8 in the morning and 5 at night in the winter, and from 7 a.m. to 10 p.m. in summer', while Marie Stopes explains how particularly fortunate her baby was, since being born in April, he had never even had a meal indoors for the first two years of his life: 'There were various sunny corners and verandas which offered shelter whatever the weather, even in January.' Prams were adapted to suit this requirement with deep sides to stop children falling out while abandoned in the garden. Cat nets and harnesses further ensured the child's safety, and when it was more active the child could be left out in a playpen – which was good for developing its self-reliance.

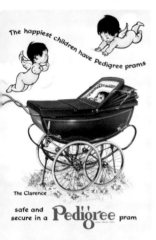

The Clarence model pram as advertised in the 1950s, designed to keep the child 'safe and secure' while it lay out in the garden.

3 A PLACE FOR FIRE AND WATER

Earth and air are the elements that are taken for granted in the garden but fire and water bring in the surprises and excitement. Fire and light at night are irresistible and even the smallest back garden can be transformed into somewhere magic with bonfires and fireworks spewing forth crackling flames and sparkling lights. Water provides reflections and glitter, soothing gurgles and splashes.

FIREWORKS

Queen Elizabeth was treated to a dramatic combination of the two elements when the Earl of Hertford entertained her at Elvetham in Hampshire in 1591. Especially for the occasion he dug out a crescent-shaped lake, complete with three islands: one a fort, one a snail mount with a spiral path and one named Ship Isle. On this he staged a mock sea battle, and afterwards, fireworks. A contemporary description recounts:

Woodcut of 'The Honourable Entertainement gieven to the Queenes Majestie in Progresse' at Elvetham, 1591. Elizabeth I under a canopy, left, watches a sea battle.

Then there was a castle of fireworkes of all sorts, which played in the fort; answerable to that there was, at the Snail Mount, a globe of all manner of fireworkes, as big as a barrel. When these were all spent there were many running rockets upon lines, which passed between the Snail Mount and the castle in the fort. On either side were many fire-wheeles, pikes of pleasure, and balles of wildfire, which burned in the water.

What adds to the excitement of fireworks and bonfires is the sense of a special occasion. Bonfires were often lit for Twelfth Night and Hallowe'en, and public fireworks marked royal births, the Lord Mayor of London's November water pageant and national victories. Samuel Pepys describes in his diary the evening of 14 August 1666 in celebration of the British navy routing the Dutch island of Schelling:

We had invited to a venison pasty Mr. Batelier and his sister Mary, Mrs. Mercer, her daughter Anne, Mr. Le Brun, and W. Hewer; and so we supped, and very merry. And then about nine o'clock to Mrs. Mercer's gate, where the fire and boys expected us, and her son had provided abundance of serpents and rockets; and there mighty merry (my Lady Pen and Pegg going thither with us, and Nan Wright), till about twelve at night, flinging our fireworks, and burning one another and the people over the way. And at last our businesses being spent, we went into Mrs. Mercer's, and there mighty merry, smutting one another with candle grease and soot, till most of us were like devils.

During the eighteenth century fireworks were a regular event at public pleasure gardens such as Ranelagh in Chelsea. Horace Walpole could see them from the garden of his Gothick Strawberry Hill in Twickenham; they added to the perfection of a June evening in 1765. He wrote in a letter to his friend George Montagu at eleven o'clock:

I am just come out of the garden on the most oriental of evenings and from breathing odours beyond those of Araby. The acacias, which the Arabians had the sense to worship, are covered with blossoms, the honeysuckles dangle from every tree in festoons, the syringas are thickets of sweets and the new cut hay of the field in the garden tempers the balmy gales with simple freshness, while a thousand sky-rockets launched into the air at Ranelagh or Marylebone illuminate the scene and give it an air of Haroun Alraschid's paradise.

Of course in Britain the combination of bonfire and fireworks is principally associated with 5 November, when the Catholic conspirator Guy Fawkes was caught lurking around with gunpowder in the cellars of the Houses of Parliament with the intention of blowing it up. Under torture he revealed the names of his co-conspirators, but it is his effigy not theirs that has been burnt annually at family parties in gardens, although in the seventeenth century the Pope was frequently burnt. William Hone describes in *The Every-Day Book*, his compendium of customs, published weekly, the mayhem of bonfire nights in 1826: 'by ten o'clock, London was so lit up by bonfires and fireworks, that from the suburbs it was in one red heat. Many were the overthrows of horsemen and carriages, from the discharge of hand-rockets, and the pressure of moving mobs inflamed to violence by drink, and fighting their way against each other.'

The golden age of British fireworks: labels from boxed selections from Standard, 1930s, and Brock's, 1950s, evoking the atmosphere of Bonfire Night.

However, by the early to mid-twentieth century Guy Fawkes Day or Bonfire Night had been domesticated. It had become

An early 1950s poster for Standard fireworks.

a family event in the back garden with toffee apples and parkin to eat, a boxed selection of fireworks to let off and a tamed bonfire. The enthusiasm for fireworks was enormous and numerous manufacturers competed for business, their advertising posters illustrating children blithely letting off fireworks at random, holding them in their hands and sticking rockets in shaky bottles. Shells – the most potentially dangerous fireworks, since they needed to be fired from a mortar – were freely available in the shop displays that ran from September. Several companies instigated children's savings clubs to ensure that pocket money was safely invested in 5 November.

John Bennett, the editor of *Fireworks Magazine*, describes firework parties in the back garden of his family's semi-detached house in Barkingside in the 1950s. He came from a family of firework enthusiasts and from an early age meticulously recorded every firework he bought in Barkingside High Street – Brock's, Wells, Standard, Wessex, Pain's, Benwell and Astra: 'Was the Wessex Gremlin the best serpent? Wessex Jack Frost the best Roman candle, or Wizard Blue Angel the best coloured fire? . . . Nearby Ilford provided bigger selections and my father and I would cycle in to make further purchases. The sound of breaking rocket sticks was, sadly, a familiar sound as we squeezed between the cars forgetting our increased width.' For bonfire night he and his brother created 'banger lairs' all the way round the garden: holes into which the bangers could be dropped with the intention of magnifying the bang. 'In those days a banger was a banger. Only the previous year, 1954, a galvanised bucket full of earth had suffered a hole through its side because it had not been removed from the table on which a modest banger had been fired.' His uncle Will would also make memorable contributions. He had a shed at the bottom of his garden where he kept flash bangers and smoke bombs left over from his wartime ARP service, during which he would simulate air raids to demonstrate what conditions would be like. On firework night he would bring some of these powerful tools into play: his 'ear-shattering explosions were in a class of their own' and he liked to end the display with a huge smoke bomb let off covertly: 'It was whilst the post-fireworks food was being devoured that a strange smell began to be noticed. Being a cold night there were few windows open and yet a smoky atmosphere soon began to permeate the house, It grew, until venturing into the garden was like walking into the worst of London's 1950 pea-soupers.'

Now it has become less acceptable to burn the effigy of a seventeenth-century committed Christian, and Guy Fawkes is no longer always found burning brightly in a discarded jacket of Father's on top of a bonfire. Bonfire Night is slowly amalgamating with Hallowe'en as the season for fireworks spreads over several weeks.

Flora Thompson, remembering her childhood in an Oxfordshire hamlet during the 1880s in *Lark Rise to Candleford*, catches the drama and excitement of lights and fire at night in a description of the family pig-killing in the garden. This happened at night – because the pork butcher, or pig-sticker, had a daytime job as a thatcher – and took place by the light of lanterns and that of the burning straw used to singe the bristles off the skin.

> The whole scene, with its mud and blood, flaring lights and dark shadows, was as savage as anything to be seen in an African jungle. The children at the end house would steal out of bed to the window. 'Look! Look! It's hell, and those are the devils,' Edmund would whisper, pointing to the men tossing the burning straw with their pitchforks; (but Laura would feel sick and would creep back into bed and cry: she was sorry for the pig.)

Fire, the most dramatic of elements when bought into the garden, has also historically caused the most contention. The sheer joy of a bonfire is well known to many gardeners, if not necessarily to their neighbours. In *Sunlight on the Lawn*, written during the 1950s, Beverley Nichols – who wrote voluminously about his various country retreats and their gardens – describes a village conflict over a bonfire between Rose and Emily; Rose stands accused of burning dead cows or poisonous chemicals or even her oldest hats, but she maintains that she is only burning up a few weeds.

> Both ladies were standing very erect, with their chins held high. It was one of the most painful moments in the whole history of Meadowstream. The conflict seemed all the sharper because of the idyllic background against which it was set. Blue skies and yellow sunshine on green grass – the scent of lavender and the hum of bees – lazy purple shadows under the limes. The only dark feature in this pastoral scene was the grey octopus of smoke that continued to weave its loathsome limbs over the laurel hedge and occasionally ... for the wind was still fickle ... stretching a peppery tentacle in our direction.

WATER

The cool of water on a hot summer's day increases the pleasure of being out in the garden, whether you merely hear the sound of it or are submerged in it. More than anything else water is associated with the idea of relaxation and peace. For that reason in *The Complete Body of Architecture* – a book many Georgians must have referred to, which pronounces on every aspect of building a fine house, including the garden – the architect Isaac Ware recommends making the most of water:

> The pleasing noise that water interrupted in its course makes, always composes the mind, fills it with the ideas of those poetical descriptions we have read, and places us in a scene with fancied nymphs and deities of the rural kind, as from immemorial time these writers have described them: it gives that cast of sedate and composed thought which makes a natural part, and a very considerable one, of

all rural enjoyment, and by the various disposition always adds a new beauty to places where it is wanted.

Water has always been a special element of gardens, from the modest spout at the centre of a medieval garden to the canals, lakes and fountains that were so favoured by owners of grand owners in the seventeenth and eighteenth centuries. As Henry Hoare wrote in a letter from Stourhead, his landscape garden in Wiltshire, during the hot summer of 1764, 'A souse in that delicious bath and grot, filld with fresh magic, is Asiatick luxury, and too much for mortals, or at least for subjects.' Now mains water, combined with plastic, concrete and electricity, means that water has become available to anyone who relishes it as part of their garden.

Engraving of Stourhead in 1777. Henry Hoare dammed the River Stour to create a lake in the 1740s. The grotto is on the far side beside the temple.

LARGE EXPANSES AND VERY SMALL

When Paul Hentzer, a German visitor to England in 1588 (travelling as a tutor to a young German nobleman), went to Lord Burghley's mansion, Theobalds, in Hertfordshire, he noted in his accounts of his travels that the garden had

> a ditch full of water, large enough for one to have the pleasure of going in a boat and rowing between the shrubs . . . we were led by the gardener into the summer-house, in the lower part of which, built semicircularly, are the twelve Roman emperors in white marble, and a table of touchstone; the upper part of it is set round with cisterns of lead, into which the water is conveyed through pipes, so that fish

The lake at West Wycombe, painted by William Hannan in the mid-eighteenth century, with a reasonably sized sailing boat. A tent has been erected on one of the islands.

may be kept in them, and in summer-time they are very convenient for bathing.

Only the very grand, such as Henry Hoare, could stretch to the creation of large spans of water. During the eighteenth century any landowner with pretensions to a fashionable landscape garden was busy damming streams and rivers to create lakes and ponds in the manner of the acknowledged master of water arrangement, Capability Brown, all of which involved having considerable manpower at your disposal. Humphry Repton wrote in *Sketches and Hints on Landscape Gardening*, 'A large lake without boats, is a dreary waste of water' and he himself organized what he called 'a peculiar ferry-boat' for those wishing to shortcut across the lake that he created in the Park at Holkham in Norfolk.

The most extreme response to seeing an expanse of water from their windows came from the group of landowners who introduced not just boats but ships in order to enjoy the sight of a good battle from the terrace. This was perhaps a logical extension of the fashion for creating small decorative fortifications in the park in the manner of the French military engineer Vauban. Mrs Delany describes in a letter a visit in October 1748 to Dangan Castle, the seat of the 'good-humoured and agreeable' Lord Mornington:

> . . . the garden (or rather improvements, and parks, for it is too extensive to be called a garden) consists of six hundred Irish acres . . . There is a gravel walk from the house to the great lake fifty-two feet broad, and six hundred yards long . . . I never saw so pretty a thing. There are several ships, one a complete man-of-war. My

godson is governor of the fort, and lord high admiral; he hoisted all his colours for my reception, and was not a little mortified that I declined the compliment of being saluted from the fort and ship.

Britain was at war in October 1748, the month of her visit.

Sir Francis Dashwood, too, offered his guests at West Wycombe the spectacle of mock naval battles fought among the four boats that he kept permanently on his lake, which was ornamented with a small fortified island. One boat was 'completely rigg'd and carries several brass carriage guns which were taken out of a French Privateer and a sailor constantly is kept who lives aboard this snow to keep it in proper order', as Thomas Phillibrown describes in his journal of 1754. He then recounts how during one sham fight the captain commanding the boat 'received damage from ye wadding of a gun which occasioned him to spit blood and so put an end to ye battle'. The 5th Lord Byron gave up his naval career when he inherited Newstead Abbey in Nottinghamshire, so possibly it was extreme frustration that led him to float six ships on his lake, including a twenty-gun schooner which he had transported overland from Hull, and surround them with a battery of four guns on the shore. In the 1760s nothing less than the 'deception of a port' would do for Matthew Fortescue on his water at Castle Hill in Devon; this, the minutes of his improvements record, he achieved by 'shredding trees' to give the impression of a small fleet of ship masts, which would have looked impressive from his sham castle on the hill. His collection of boats included a schooner, a skiff, and a wherry with an awning to give it the appearance of a gondola.

The vogue for chinoiserie was also a stimulus. Junks, bridges, inland seas and islets were favourite motifs in almost any piece of chinoiserie design. The Duke of Cumberland's house at Virginia Water had a famed Chinese junk on it and when Richard Pococke went there in August 1754 he described in his travel journal what he saw on the small lake: 'a small yacht, which has sailed on the sea, a Chinese ship, the middle of which is high, covered and glazed, a Venetian gondola, and five or six other different kinds of boats'. For a quick effect the boat did not actually have to move, but just be yet another amusing spot from which to enjoy the garden.

Ranelagh Gardens opened in 1742 and soon had the attraction of a floating chinoiserie pavilion on an ornamental lake beside its famous rotunda. The Halfpenny brothers published a *Country Gentleman's Pocket Companion and Builder's Assistant*: a small optimistic book with inexpensive suggestions, including designs for floats – garden buildings to be moored permanently on a lake or pond offering the opportunity for people to recreate a London pleasure garden experience at home.

The Victorian male was pleased to row or punt about a lake of any size, demonstrating his prowess to women obediently installed under a sun shade in the stern. A clandestine outing in a boat is recorded in the diary of James Lewis, a footman in the Duchess of Sutherland's household. In September 1838, he got up at dawn to sneak a row on the lake at Trentham, the family's country house in Staffordshire: 'The night porter called me this morning about 5. I got up at half past and started to go on the pleasure grounds and went to the boat house and found the boats unlocked so we took one and went out on the water for an hour,' an escapade which he repeats several times during his visit.

Chromolithograph of punting on the lake at Trentham, published in *The Gardens of England* by E. Adveno Brooke, twenty years after James Lewis rowed there at dawn.

FISH

The fish in monastic stew ponds were strictly water larders, but when Izaak Walton wrote the *Compleat Angler*, subtitled *The Contemplative Man's Recreation*, in 1653 it was in response to the zeitgeist. Walton quoted Sir Henry Wotton, another angler, describing fishing as 'an employment of idle time, which was not then idly

63

Detail of men fishing from the bird's-eye view of the garden of a house called Little Offley, from Chauncy's *Historical Antiquities of Hertfordshire*, 1700.

spent . . . a cheerer of spirits, a diverter of sadness, a calmer of unquiet thoughts, a moderator of passions'. John Evelyn diverted water at his brother George's house at Wotton to create 'stews and receptacles for fish', and later at his own house at Sayes Court in Deptford stocked water for his son-in-law William Draper to fish. Little pavilions were built beside ponds and lakes for solitude and fishing.

Few gardens of the late Victoria or Edwardian era were without their lily ponds or reflecting pools and these remained popular features into the twentieth century, easily reproduced with the help of a bag or ready-mixed concrete or, subsequently, black plastic sheeting. Few garden ponds lack fish. P.G. Wodehouse in *Right Ho, Jeeves*, written in the early 1920s, endows the character of Gussie Fink-Nottle with a passion for his garden pond that would have struck a chord with the readers of *The Aquarist and Pondkeeper* magazine, which was founded in 1928 to appeal to an enthusiastic and growing audience, and in which one of its contributors wrote: 'On a wet day it soothes, as the rain-drops weave gauzy patterns on the surface and the fish dart to and fro.' Bertie Wooster describes Gussie: 'He lived year in and year out, covered with moss, in a remote village in Lincolnshire, never coming up even for the Eton and Harrow Match. And when I asked him once if he didn't find the time hang a bit heavy on his hands, he said, no, because he had a pond in his garden and studied the habits of newts!'

This garden pastime, as with so many to do with water, seemed firmly in the hands of men, as George F. Hervey and Jack Hems, the authors of a modest 1958 *Book of the Garden Pond*, stated: 'Our audience

Water devices (above and right) from John Bate, *The Mysteryes of Nature and Art*, 1634. Here, water spouts out of a sounding trumpet.

64

is the man of modest means, the do-it-yourself man to appropriate as an adjective the current fashionable term.'

WATER JOKES

The piping of water was an exciting new technology in the seventeenth century, directing water to wherever it was wanted – the house, a fountain or into a pool. Complicated hydraulics were a major feature of Italian sixteenth- and seventeenth-century gardens and, as with other fashions, imported into Britain. The craze for creating effects to bring an element of surprise and shock to a simple walk round the garden seems to have entranced the nation for at least two centuries. Paul Hentzer saw them at Theobalds in the reign of Queen Elizabeth: 'In the garden joining to this palace there is a jet d'eau, with a sun-dial, which while strangers are looking at, a quantity of water, forced by a wheel which the gardener turns at a distance, through a number of small pipes, plentifully sprinkles those that are standing round.'

Bate's diagram of 'how to make that a bird sitting on a sis, shall make a noise, and drink out of a cup of water, being held to the mouth of it.'

Celia Fiennes comments several times on such elaborate water schemes in the accounts that she gave of her journeys round Britain on horseback in the following century. At Wilton, in Wiltshire, she saw the famous waterworks created for the 4th Earl of Pembroke in the 1630s: 'The river runs through the garden that easily conveys by pipes water to all parts. A Grottoe is at the end of the garden just the middle off the house, its garnished with many fine figures of the Goddesses, and about 2 yards off the doore is severall pipes in a line that with a sluce spouts water up to wett the Strangers.' At Chatsworth, which she visited in 1697, she saw an equally complicated diversion, which she describes rather breathlessly:

There is another greene walke and about the middle of it by the Grove stands a fine Willow tree, the leaves and barke and all looks very naturall, the roote is full of rubbish or great stones to appearance, and all on a sudden by turning a sluce it raines from each leafe and from the branches like a shower, it being made of brass and pipes to each leafe but in appearance is exactly like any Willow; beyond this is a bason in which are the branches of two Hartichocks Leaves which weeps at the end of each leafe into the bason which is placed at the foote of lead steps 30 in number, the lowest step is very deep and between every 4 stepps is a half pace all made of lead and are broad on each side, on a little banck stands blew balls 10 on a side, and between each ball are 4 pipes which by a sluce spouts out water across the stepps to each other like an arbour or arch; while you are thus amused suddenly there runs down a torrent of water out of 2 pitchers in the hands of two large Nimphs cut in stone that lyes in the upper step.

The novelty and amusement to be had from these water jokes must have worn exceptionally thin by the time visitors and friends were taken round Dyrham, Mr Blaythwayte's garden near Bath, described by Stephen Switzer in *The Nobleman, Gentleman, and Gardener's Recreation* in 1742. Here, disguised pipes were run into a tree, under which was placed a tempting seat. He could then surprise his guests as they stopped for a rest by turning a stopcock and drenching them: 'the more these pipes have play'd, the closer they have embrac'd the tree for shelter; supposing it had really rain'd, till the Gardener has convinc'd them of their Error.' However, finally the fun of 'Wetting Strangers' was over and the persuasive Isaac Ware urged the removal of all remaining evidence of 'foul bason half filled with stinking water, green with over-growing moss and the habitation of newts and frogs'.

How to swim backstroke: explanatory woodcut from *De Arte Natandi*.

The pleasure of jets of water, well aimed or misdirected, can just be detected in J.C. Loudon's early Victorian gardening compendium, *The Suburban Gardener and Villa Companion*. 'And what can be more rational than the satisfaction which the grown up amateur, or master of the house, enjoys, when he returns from the city to his garden in the summer evenings, and applies the syringe to his wall trees, with refreshing enjoyment to himself and the plants, and to the delight of his children, who may be watching his operations?' The rubber watering hose was a new invention and surely it wasn't used only for watering plants.

The master, his daughter and the gardener all enthusiastically using Vulcanized India Rubber Hose, manufactured by H. Statham & Co. Manchester: advertisement, *c.*1885.

How to swim sidestroke, from *De Arte Natandi*.

PLUNGING IN

The earliest British swimming manual was *De Arte Natandi*, written in 1587 by Everard Digby, fellow of St John's College Cambridge, who presumably practised his strokes in the shallow River Cam. Less than ten years later a translation from the Latin appeared, which points out the obvious truth that learning to swim might save one's life 'from the greedy jaws of the swelling sea' and then describes the joys: 'it is a thing necessary for every man to use, even in the pleasantest and securest time of his life, especially as the fittest thing to purge the skin from all external pollutions or uncleanness whatsoever, as sweat and such like, as also it helpeth to temperate the extreme heat of the body in the burning time of the year.' Swimming was principally a masculine occupation and among the list of attributes considered by Sir Henry Peacham as requisite for being a complete gentleman.

His contemporary Francis Bacon did not need to follow Digby's advice on finding a safe riverbank from which to swim (watching out for stinging serpents and poisoned toads), being in a position to create a swimming pool in his own garden. In his essay 'Of Gardens' he suggests building a 'bathing pool' of some 'thirty or forty foot square, but without fish, or slime, or mud'. Instead he wanted 'the bottom finely paved, and with images; the sides likewise; and withal embellished with coloured glass, and such things of lustre'. In a way that sounds distinctly modern, he wanted the water to be in perpetual motion, 'fed by water higher than the pool, and delivered into it by fair spouts, and then discharged away under ground'. The pool's decoration evidently absorbed him and John Aubrey recounted later in *Brief Lives* how 'if a poore bodie had brought his Lordship half a dozen pebbles of a curious colour, he would give them a shilling.'

Watercolour of Richard Payne Knight, poet, connoisseur and enthusiast of the picturesque, sitting beside his 'Roman' bath house at Downton Castle, *c*.1800.

Dipping into water for health was partly the point of spas such as Bath, and during the eighteenth century sea bathing too became fashionable. Setting up a system for plunging into cold water for both health and pleasure in your own garden was a natural development. Baths, as well as grottoes, cascades and fountains, were all watery features that the landscape gardener and architect Batty Langley advertised as his area of expertise during the 1720s; his advice might be 'readily commanded at all times to any part of Great Britain or Ireland'. Organizing water was a serious business, damming, diverting and channelling requiring expertise and resources. Garden baths in all likelihood were intended mainly for men and involved small buildings set over pools of cold water into which they could plunge. However, a remark in Richard Pococke's journal recording a visit to Marston in July 1754 suggests that possibly women also enjoyed a quick dip: 'Two or three fields below the house is a cold bath, as in an enclosure of an ancient Cimitery, with several old inscriptions made for it, and at the end is a small room very elegantly furnished, this I take to be Lady Orrery's place of retirement.' David Garrick converted a riverside cottage into a bath house at his house in Hampton on the Thames.

As with other incidental garden buildings, the bath could appear as an ornamental architectural feature, perhaps combined with a grotto or even, as William Wrighte illustrated in *Grotesque Architecture or Rural Amusement* (1767), as part of a hermitage in the 'Augustine Stile' which linked two circular retreats, one a library and the other a bath with niches for seats cut from an evergreen screen. He notes: 'if the water in the plan is to be left out, it will look very pleasing as a rural hut'. The building would usually have had seats both inside, for the 'conveniency of dressing and undressing', and outside, for warming up afterwards. 'As clear as crystal and as cold as ice' was how the bath chamber built for the Earl of Lincoln at Oatlands in Surrey was described. This, decorated entirely in shells, was part of an elaborate grotto that also included a gaming room. Started in 1747, at great cost (£40,000) it included a statue of Venus de Medici.

Mrs Delany was well known for her decorative shellwork decoration. She wrote in a letter in June 1750 of a commission she had had from a local worthy who was altering his garden and wanted her to decorate part of his bath: 'but I cannot say he has shown so much real judgement as *conceit* in what he has done. In one part of the garden there is a cold bath that opens with an arch like a cave, this is put under my care to adorn and make something of, and I have presumed to undertake it. When finished I'll send you a little sketch of it.' Two weeks later she described spending a very rainy day with the Vesey family at Lucan near Dublin, where she was entertained in various garden buildings, including surprisingly, the bath. They had breakfast in Mrs Vesey's dairy, 'the table *strewed with roses*', and later 'we dined in the cold bath – I mean in its antichamber; it was as pleasant as a rainy day could be when we wanted to roam about.'

A bath for the garden was one of the projects J.B. Papworth proposed in his Regency pattern book, *Hints on Ornamental Gardening* (1823). He extols the delights of bathing just for the joy of it, an innocent pleasure. 'A Bath should not be neglected, for its important usefulness demands a place wherever pure water can be obtained; and the agreeableness alone of bathing, without its salubrity, should suffice to procure to the bath a higher degree of patronage than it has yet received in this country.' He blames bathing's lack of popularity on the impediment of powdered hair: 'during many years the difficulties of dress, consequent on the fashion of wearing powder in the hair, were inimical to its use: this impediment being removed, it is probable that baths will be employed by us as common and frequent sources of innocent pleasure as well as for medical relief.'

Fanny Hill, John Cleland's wanton heroine in *Memoirs of a Woman of Pleasure* (1749), found bathing an enticing experience. She describes a riverside episode one fine summer day with her friend Emily and their two gallants:

> After tea, and taking a turn in the garden, my particular, who was the master of the house, and had in no sense schem'd that this party of pleasure for a dry one, propos'd to us, as the weather was excessively hot, to bathe together, under a commodious shelter that he had prepared expressly for that purpose, in a creek of the river . . . Emily who never refused anything, and I, who ever delighted in bathing, and had no exception to the person who proposed it, or to those pleasures it was easy to guess that it implied . . . without loss of time, we returned instantly to the pavilion, one door of which open'd into a tent, pitch'd before it, that with its marquise, formed a pleasing defense against the sun, or the weather, and was besides as private as we could wish. The lining of it, emboss'd cloth, represented a wild, forest-foliage, from the top, down to the sides, which, in the same stuff, were figur'd with fluted pilasters, with their spaces between fill'd with flower-vases, the whole having a gay effect upon the eye,

wherever you turn'd it. Then it reached sufficiently into the water, yet contained convenient benches round it on the dry ground, either to keep our clothes, or . . . or . . . in short for more uses than resting upon. There was a side-table too, loaded with sweetmeats, jellies, or other eatables, and bottles of wine and cordials, by way of occasional relief from any rawness, or chill of the water, or from any faintness from whatever cause.

Men swam naked but for women, other than Fanny, there had to be elaborate systems of modesty. At the seaside bathing was done from the privacy of a machine drawn out into the waves. Families bathing from their own riversides made alternative arrangements. In 1800 on 14 August Caroline Lybbe Powys, while staying with her daughter, watched her bathe in the river with the grandchildren: 'I walked down to the river Blyth by seven in the morn to see Caroline and the three eldest children bathe, which they did most mornings, having put up a dressing-house on the bank,' she recorded in her diary. But the experience of swimming was rare.

The swimming volume of the *Badminton Library of Sports and Pastimes* noted as late as 1908 that women needed privacy to swim: 'There are not many lady swimmers who bathe in open fresh water, privacy being somewhat difficult to obtain.' Someone who had solved the problem was 'Mrs. Cecile Samuda, who bathes all through the summer in a large deep lake in the gardens at her residence, Shipton Court, Oxon'. The indomitable Mrs Samuda apparently organized a week of competitions at the end of each swimming season: 'the hostess acts a judge, allows each competitor three fair trials, her brother undertaking the duties of starter.' When the doyenne of English garden designers Gertrude Jekyll wrote on the subject of *Wall and Water Gardens* in 1901 she remarked that some large houses had bathing pools, and she could well see the attraction. 'A bath in running water in the early sunlight of our summer days would be a much appreciated addition to the delights of many a good garden' and she could imagine something beautiful along the lines of the Villa d'Este: 'a long swimming-pool, the lower end in sunlight; the upper giving access to a small building, perhaps of classical design, standing in a grove of ilex'.

In the first half of the twentieth century private swimming pools were rare luxuries. They were square and concrete and had to be laboriously emptied and cleaned when they became green and soupy. They were also the perfect backdrop for sunbathing. Pools with rectilinear concrete lines or clear curved shapes fitted well with modernist architecture, although such houses were rare in Britain. A low-maintenance weekend retreat in Cobham, Surrey, with a garden scheme by landscape architect Christopher Tunnard was illustrated in his 1938 book *Gardens in the Modern Landscape*: 'A combined swimming-pool and boating-lake is flanked by a sandy foreshore for sunbathing' and is complete with a springboard for diving. When Eric Ravilious designed a service for Wedgwood on the theme of 'The Garden' in 1938 he included a man diving into a swimming pool, which may have been the reason why he was informed that the design was not very accessible to the British public.

Gordon Cullen's illustration of the swimming pond designed by Christopher Tunnard for the Surrey garden of a modernist house.

Swimming pool culture came to Britain from the carefree and glamorous West Coast of America; fifties magazines ran countless issues featuring Hollywood film stars lounging around their Californian pools, which showed how life could be lived in the garden, given unlimited money and sunshine. Thomas Church, an influential American garden designer, wrote in his 1955 book *Gardens are for People*: 'The private swimming pool (gunite [sprayed concrete] and plastic), once a luxury for the few, seems to be here to stay for many. The pool is a place to gather around, much as a fireplace in a room.' It was Church who pioneered the free-form kidney-shaped pool.

He told of a world of floating trays for martinis, poolside cabanas with space for dressing rooms, filter and heating equipment, electrical outlets for refrigerator, percolator, radio and TV, and a jack for a telephone, all of which would have been an impossible dream for the average Briton living under conditions of post-war austerity.

Changes are reflected in the famous advertisements of *Country Life* for desirable country houses. They started in January 1944 and early examples typically include a garden with 'Beautiful pleasure grounds, including topiary and other ornamental gardens, bowling green, hard and grass tennis courts, woodland gardens studded with rare trees and flowering shrubs, walled kitchen garden, two fine drive entrances, stabling and loose boxes for over 30 horses'; by the 1960s advertisements were more likely to include 'squash court, swimming pool, studio or games room, charming gardens and grounds with tennis court, garaging for 5 cars and 2 paddocks'.

Swimming pools were still exotic in the early 1960s and became loosely associated with notorious events such as those that took place at Cliveden, Lord Astor's country house, on one exceptionally hot July weekend in 1961 and which had repercussions far beyond Berkshire. Christine Keeler (teenage topless dancer) revealed in the *Sunday Pictorial* that she had been chased naked round the floodlit swimming pool by a dinner-jacketed John Profumo (Minister for War). It was at night in a West Sussex pool in 1969 that Rolling Stone Brian Jones died. However, as the 1960s gave way to the 1970s the swimming pool, with water filtered, heated and made 'mediterranean blue' by its mosaic lining, became increasingly attainable.

The most recent garden addition is the hot tub spa, intended to soothe away the stress of life and for leaping into after a hard day at the office – a cedar-clad barrel, in 'private or party size', with whirlpool effects to aid relaxation. These were the invention of American Roy Jacuzzi, who

RUTHERFORD

Have fun
in your
Rutherford
Swimming Pool

—with sparkling
heated water—

a pool built
by experts
for you to enjoy

For details of our Swimming Pools,
Diatomite Filters, Solar Heaters
and Accessories, contact:

RUTHERFORD CONSTRUCTION CO. LTD
BATTLE, SUSSEX, ENGLAND BATTLE 468 (4 lines) ASCOT 199

Once heating systems were put in place, the British swimming pool could be advertised in a more glamorous fashion: 1950s.

in 1968 incorporated water pumps originally designed as hydrotherapy into the sides of an ordinary bath, and then in 1970 further advanced the idea by producing a heated garden model. He may not have been thinking about classical nymphs and deities as Isaac Ware did, but his first effort was marketed as a 'Roman Bath' and his double version was called 'The Adonis'.

4   A PLACE TO SIT IN SUN AND SHADE

Sitting out in the garden might involve sleeping, daydreaming, reading, talking, working or just existing; eyes might be open to every detail of the immediate surroundings or distant views, or they might be shut. It might be a way of filling a day, the garden a place for a few minutes' respite or a place to do household chores. A beautiful day in 1450 would elicit, one assumes, exactly the same response as a beautiful day in 1950 – an urgent desire to escape the house into warmth and sunshine and then to sit and enjoy it.

TURF BENCHES AND ARBOURS

We have a vision of the medieval enclosed garden from painting and literature: a small green world of flower-dotted grass. Around the edge of the garden are turf benches, held in place with wattles or wooden boards; as a backdrop trellis or walls with climbing plants. The sitter faces inwards to a central tree or simple water feature. Chaucer evoked such a garden in *Troilus and Criseyde*. It was 'large and railed', with the paths or alleys 'shadowed well with blossomy boughs green,/And benched new, and sanded all the ways.' La bell Pucel, the golden-haired heroine of Stephen Hawes' poem 'The History of Graunde Amoure', sits alone, 'amiddes an harber' making a garland of flowers:

Late fifteenth-century woodcut:
a woman on a grassy bench.

To Paradise, right well comparable
Set about with floures fragrant,
And in the middle, there was resplendishaunt
A dulcet spring, and marvylous fountain
Of gold and asure, made all certaine . . .
Beside whiche fountaine, the most fayre lady
La bell Pucell, was gayly sitting.

An arbour gave shade, seen as essential by the Tudor doctor Andrew Boorde, who advised: 'In summer keep your neck and face from the sun; use to wear gloves made of goat-skin, perfumed with ambergis. And beware in standing or

A woodcut from Thomas Hill's *The Gardeners' Labyrinth*, 1577, of men building an arbour complete with benches and table, the bright sun demonstrating the need for shade.

lying on the ground in the reflection of the sun, but be moveable.' But equally, and perhaps more typically given British summers, arbours could, in John Worlidge's words, be 'moist and foul' and 'apt to impair your health'. He continued: 'they are draughty, and on a hot day it is pleasanter to sit under a lime tree than to be hoodwinked in an arbour.' The turf seat lingered on beyond the medieval period and in *The Country Housewife's Garden* (1618) William Lawson was still recommending them: 'In all your gardens and orchards, banks and seats of camomile, penny-royal, daisies and violets are seemly and comfortable.' Both camomile and penny royal are aromatic when crushed, so scent would have added further pleasure to sitting outside.

SITTING AND LOOKING OUT

The defensible inward-looking medieval garden faded from fashion as the world outside became a safer place. People wanted to look out from their gardens, or at least over them. For this purpose the mount was a favourite seventeenth- and early eighteenth-century feature, its summit the perfect place to sit. 'Raise a mount with waste earth or rubbish you may otherwise happen to be troubled withal at some convenient distance from your House . . . you have the advantage of Air and Prospect' was John Worlidge's advice. The mount's fall from fashion peeved the poet Anne Finch, Countess of Winchelsea, who in the early eighteenth century was moved to verse when her husband swept away her favourite seat at Eastwell in Kent, writing in 'Upon my Lord Winchilsea's Converting the Mount in his Garden to a Terrace':

> So lies this hill, hewn from its rugged height,
> Now leveled to a scene of smooth delight,
> Where on a terrace of its spoils we walk,
> And of the task, and the performer talk, . . .
> Where late it stood, the glory of the seat,
> Repelled the winter blasts, and screened the summer's heat;
> So praised, so loved, that when untimely fate)
> Sadly prescribed it a too early date,
> The heavy tidings cause a general grief.

A few remained in place, and Stephen Switzer was impressed by the mount in Mr Blaythwayt's garden, which makes allowances for the weather: 'you advance to a Mount . . . on top of which is a large seat, call'd a *Windsor* Seat, which is contriv'd to turn around any Way, either for the Advantage of the Prospect, or to avoid the Inconvenience of Wind, the Sun etc,' he wrote in *The Nobleman, Gentleman, and Gardener's Recreation.*

Isaac Ware in *The Complete Body of Architecture* (1756) declared garden seats, or 'conveniences of repose', to be essential – and gave guidance to the Georgian garden owner. 'It would be absurd to terminate a vast walk with a plain bench, nor less ridiculous to erect a pompous temple where there was not an extent of 100 yds. from the building.' For town gardens, best paved, he also gave consideration to putting enough distance between the privy and where one might sit in the garden for enjoyment. The 'needful edifice' should be placed in the farthest corner, and balanced by a matching shed in the other corner, but it was important to avoid the mistake, commonly made, of putting an alcove with a seat between the two: 'a strange place to sit for pleasure'. Generally the advice was to disguise the convenience with honeysuckle and virgin's bower – clematis. Horace Walpole in a letter of 1753 describes a bishop's palace he had seen as 'having a small pert portico, like the conveniences at the end of a London garden'. Privies would

Humphry Repton's view from his Essex cottage garden, with its outlook
of the busy high road, 'which I would not exchange for any of the lonely parks
that I have improved for others'.

have been emptied by night, often through the house, by the literally
named nightman.

The pleasure of sitting in a garden and watching the world beyond go
by is immutable. Many garden gazebos of the seventeenth and eighteenth
centuries were placed at the edges of gardens, overlooking the public
highway. Isaac Ware wrote that 'a road at a proper distance, or a navigable
river, affords a continual moving picture . . . Retirement is what we seek
in the country, but it must not be too absolute. Company in the country
is as medicine.' Humphry Repton reiterated this view in *Sketches and
Hints* when commenting on his improvement at Endsleigh in Devon: 'It
is hardly necessary to remark how much the view from the house would
be enlivened by the smoke of a cottage on the opposite side of the water'
or better still a mill with 'busy motion of persons'. In the design that he
did for a workhouse in Kent, Repton pointed out how cheerful it would be
for the old inmates to sit on their sunny south-facing terrace and how 'the
view of the Country will be delightful; since the immediate fore-ground
consists of a garden, and the perpetually varying and moving scene which

is represented by the great road to Canterbury, and the Coast'. Dorothy Wordsworth mentions in her journal sitting on the Dove Cottage garden wall and enjoying the site of a landau emblazoned with a coronet driving by. 'The ladies (evidently Tourists) turned an eye of interest upon our little garden and cottage.' Sadly this interchange of mutual interest was lost when the noise and speed of traffic prevented the onlookers engaging with the passers-by and vice versa.

AVOIDING THE SUN

The sun was 'an Inconvenience' to being in the garden. In *The New Principles of Gardening* Batty Langley was didactic on the subject of shade: 'There is nothing more agreeable in a Garden than good *shade,* and without it *a garden is nothing.*' His ideal garden design, for 1723, included cool wildernesses and groves, but to reach them it was important to create avenues of trees leading to them so that 'we might with Pleasure pass and repass at any time of Day' and avoid what he termed the scorching heat of the sun. Eighteenth-century dress clearly did not lend itself to remaining cool in the sunshine, but the unknown lady from Lincolnshire who enthused to Dr Johnson on the delights of being in a shady grotto on a summer day was famously rebuffed with the statement that the Englishman 'has more frequent need to solicit than exclude the sun' and that grottoes were more suited to toads. However, if Dr Johnson searched out time in the sun, he was unusual.

In *Mansfield Park* Fanny Price expresses precisely the view of an early nineteenth-century girl when she remarks: 'to sit in the shade on a fine day, and look upon verdure, is the most perfect refreshment'. Later she gets a headache from picking roses in direct sun. Edmund is concerned:

> 'Did you go out in the heat?'
>
> 'Go out! to be sure she did,' said Mrs Norris; 'would you have her stay within on such a fine day as this? Were not we *all* out? Even your mother was out today for above an hour.'
>
> 'Yes, indeed, Edmund,' added her ladyship, who had been thoroughly awakened by Mrs Norris's sharp reprimand to Fanny; 'I

was out above an hour. I sat three quarters of an hour in the flower garden, while Fanny cut the roses, and very pleasant it was I assure you, but very hot. It was shady enough in the alcove, but I declare I quite dreaded the coming home again.'

'Fanny has been cutting roses, has she?'

'Yes, and I am afraid they will be the last this year. Poor thing! *She* found it hot enough, but they were so full blown, that one could not wait.'

'There was no help for it certainly,' rejoined Mrs Norris in rather a softened voice; 'but I question whether her headach might not be caught *then*, sister. There is nothing so likely to give it as standing and stooping in a hot sun. But I dare say it will be well tomorrow. Suppose you let her have your aromatic vinegar; I always forget to have mine filled.' . . .

'I am afraid it was, indeed,' said the more candid Lady Bertram, who had overheard her; 'I am very much afraid she caught the headach there, for the heat was enough to kill anybody. It was as much as I could bear myself. Sitting and calling to Pug, and trying to keep him from the flower-beds, was almost too much for me.'

FROM SHADE TO SUN

In the early twentieth century the benefits of sunshine to health began to be understood, when it was discovered that Vitamin D could be absorbed through the skin. After centuries of seeking out the shade, however, it was felt necessary to explain how to approach the sun. An early BBC publication, *Home, Health, and Garden*, an anthology of household talks given during 1927, includes a talk given by Dr Caleb Saleeby called 'How to Take a Sunbath'. 'In the first place, the sun must be shining,' he begins, and he continues:

A mother holds her child up to the elements: cover of a BBC booklet.

Next, the skin must be released; otherwise we are merely bathing our clothes . . . It is worth while to remind women, and even men when, for once, they can appear in a shirt without a coat, that artificial silk for stockings, tennis shirts and so forth, admits more ultra-violet light than any other material of which clothes can be made; but it must be white or as nearly so as possible. Next the rule is *hasten slowly*. The unaccustomed skin must learn to use its liberty. Blisters and long-lasting redness must be avoided. There is nothing during the bath to tell us that we are getting too large a dose.

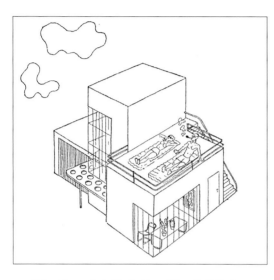

Osbert Lancaster's illustration of Twentieth-Century Functional, 'a house fit for purposes such as sun-bathing, which the English climate and environment frequently rendered impossible of fufilment', 1938.

Sunbathing was a solution for 'Diseases of darkness', such as tuberculosis, and 'the new practice, as old as Hippocrates, which uses the breath and the light of Heaven, cures them'.

With the servant problem growing, being tanned now indicated a life of leisure rather than work, whereas for earlier generations to be brown was a sign of a life of toil. There was, however, nervousness about the effects of sunbathing; magazine beauty articles of the 1930s issued warnings in this vein:

In this indolent weather it is a temptation to lie for hours like lizards in the sun. A warm glowing brown colour has its allure. But the older woman should think twice before starting a drastic baking process. Her skin is very apt to take on a dried-out, weather-beaten look, which is neither pretty nor becoming, and which may be permanently injurious. Most women over thirty-five are recognising their limitations.

This volte-face caused the older Edwardian generation to feel shock, and to some extent repulsion. E.F. Benson created the character of Isabel Poppet in *Mapp and Lucia*: 'turned black with all those sun-baths, and her hair spiky and wiry with so many sea-baths, Isabel resembled a cross between a kipper and a sea-urchin.' Or 'Her hair was like a twisted mop, her skin incredibly tanned, and mounted on her cycle she looked like a sort of modernized Valkyrie in rather bad repair.'

SITTING DRAMATICALLY AND PICTURESQUELY

As well as the formal seat and shady alcove Georgians were attracted to the idea of including a bit of wilderness in their immediate surroundings. Alexander Pope had a wild zone in his famous garden at Twickenham in the mid-eighteenth century, described in a report on the January 1748 issue of the *Newcastle General Magazine*:

> Among the Hillocks on the upper Part of the open Area, rises a Mount much higher than the rest, and is composed of more rude and indigested materials; it is covered with Bushes and Trees of a wilder Growth, and more confused Order, rising as it were out of a Clef of Rock and Heaps of rugged and mossy Stones; where is placed a Forest Seat or Chair, that may hold three or four persons at once, overshaded with the Branches of a spreading Tree.

From W. & J. Halfpenny's *The Country Gentleman's Pocket Companion*, 1758

A forest chair was something rustic and chosen to complement rock and moss. Mrs Delany described such a thing in her Dublin garden when writing to her sister in 1744:

Charles Over's suggestion for a 'Rustic Seat' composed of precariously arranged rocks, from his book *Ornamental Architecture*, 1758.

> There are several prettinesses I can't explain to you – little wild walks, private seats, and

lovely prospects. One seat I am particularly fond of, in a nut grove, and '*the beggar's hut*,' which is a seat in a rock; on top are bushes of all kinds that bend over; it is placed at the end of a cunning wild path, thick set with trees, and it overlooks the brook, which entertains you with a purling rill. The little robins are as fond of the seat as we are; it just holds the Dean and myself.

Lady Luxborough was desperate to have a moss seat and implored William Shenstone in a letter: 'Pray let me know how you make your *Moss-seats*; I want some such greatly in my coppice.' His silence on the matter infuriated her: 'Pray, pray let somebody tell my servant how your little moss-seats are made.'

The Herefordshire landowner Richard Payne Knight was an enthusiast for picturesque scenery and explained exactly how it should look in 'The Landscape', a poem he wrote in 1794:

> The cover'd seat, that shelter from the storm,
> May oft' a feature of the landscape form;
> Whether, compos'd of native stumps and roots,
> It spreads the creeper's rich fantastic shoots;
> Or rais'd with stones, irregularly pil'd,
> It seems some cavern desolate and wild.

The desire to achieve a picturesque scene encouraged landowners of the early nineteenth century to rearrange not only their own but also other people's gardens – those of their tenants. A favourite addition was the rustic seat on which a labourer would be seen taking his rest. The title of Edmund Bartell's 1804 book set the tone – *Hints for Picturesque Improvements in Ornamented Cottages, and their Scenery: including some Observations on the Labourer and his Cottage* – and he suggested 'rude stone, the root of a tree, or a piece of plank supported by frosts . . . the seat should be useful, but nothing more'. Richard Brown in *Domestic Architecture* (1842) believed that rural cottages should be designed with a veranda along the outside, shelter against the summer heat; here 'the occupant may take his exercise, read and meditate quietly, or with his family sit on rustic seats and enjoy the beauties of nature which surround their dwelling.'

The reality was that many, in particular women, were likely to be making use of the bright light of outdoors to sew, spin or knit, as Dorothy Wordsworth did one day in August 1800, writing in her journal: 'A very fine evening. I sate on the wall making my shifts until I could see no longer.' Women industriously at work outside their cottage doors were a popular theme for artists from George Morland to Helen Allingham, based on observation. The sunny cottage exteriors painted in picturesque decay were in contrast to what were in truth dark, damp and smoky interiors. Many women augmented the family income by working in rural industries and in order to be as productive as possible they used the light outside. Lace making, glove making, stocking knitting and straw plaiting were all craft skills that

demanded close attention to detail. Two plates in *The Young Tradesman* published in 1839 show both the Lacemaker and the Spinner working outside: 'The lacemaker is represented busily engaged in her work in the open air, which, even in this country, is no uncommon sight during the summer months.'

In *Lark Rise to Candleford* Flora Thompson describes Queenie, a bobbin lace maker 'brought up to the pillow', who remembered when lace making was a regular industry in the hamlet, and how 'In the summer they would sit in the shade behind one of the "housen", and as they gossiped, the bobbins flew

Romanticized engravings of women from *The Young Tradesma*. making best use of daylight out of doors to get their work finished.

and the lovely delicate pattern lengthened until the piece was completed and wrapped in blue paper and stored away to wait the great day when the year's work was taken to Banbury Fair and sold to the dealer.'

It follows that William Morris, with his belief in the value of craft, should have created at Red House in Kent, built during the 1850s, a porch especially intended for sitting and working in. For the house's interior he designed embroidered hangings that were to be hand-stitched and much of the work was done by his wife Janey, who presumably worked long hours in the porch as Morris intended. Even in 1969 when heat and light had been long taken for granted, the garden designer John Brookes considered in *Room Outside* that a normal housewife 'might more pleasantly do much of her housework in a well-designed garden when the weather is fine – sewing, shelling peas and ironing'.

GEORGIAN PATTERNS, UMBRELLAS AND TENTS

Toiling in the garden was not what Georgian garden owners did: they planned, directed and designed, and they had time and inclination to

Two of Robert Manwaring's designs for rural living: a garden seat and a pair of chairs.

sit, view, admire and make conversation. They commissioned paintings of themselves sitting and talking in their gardens. Sometimes it is clear that good furniture has been removed from the house, but in others the furniture was evidently specifically intended for the garden. Pale-painted Windsor chairs were easily produced by a carpenter or joiner and these were joined by a range of more sophisticated designs as the pattern book trade responded to demand.

For furnishing summer houses and garden temples Robert Manwaring designed 'very rich and elegant rural chairs', which in his 1765 *The Cabinet and Chair-Maker's Real Friend and Companion* he claimed were 'the only ones of the kind that ever were published'; he hoped they would give 'general satisfaction with respect to their Grandeur, Variety, Novelty and Usefulness; and that if I succeed in this Point, I shall think myself amply satisfied with the Time and Trouble I have been at composing them.' Some of his designs were of standard chair shapes appropriately carved with shepherds, flowers, reapers and fountains, but others were faux rustic, appearing to be fashioned from boughs of yew, apple or pear and painted with leaves and blossom. If natural wooden branches were well seasoned and available, and the bark peeled off, he thought these too would serve. It was self-promoting nonsense that Manwaring was the first to publish garden furniture designs, since Thomas Chippendale had published some three years earlier his pattern book *The Gentleman and Cabinet-Maker's Director*, which included chairs for arbours and summer houses, their backs ornamented with a carved trophy composed of garden tools.

Such fine pieces of furniture were likely to be found in garden buildings of the sort created at Hampton by the actor David Garrick and his wife, who built a classical rotunda temple on the edge of the Thames in anticipation of the bicentenary of Shakespeare's birth – Garrick's fame and vast fortune rested principally on his Shakespearean roles. Mrs Delany described in a letter a visit in 1770:

The Garricks with their dogs, painted by Johann Zoffany outside the Shakespeare Temple c.1762. His neighbour, Horace Walpole, helped with the exterior planting and offered cypresses.

> We had an excellent dinner nicely served, and then went over directly into the garden – a piece of irregular ground sloping down to the Thames, very well laid out, and planted for shade and shelter; and an opening to the river which appears beautiful from that spot, and from Shakespeare's Temple at the end of the Improvement, where we drank tea, and where there is a very fine statue of Shakespeare in white marble, and a great chair with a large carved frame, that was Shakespeare's own chair, made for him on some particular occasion, with a medallion fixed in the back. Many were the relics we saw of the favourite poet. At six o'clock Lady Weymouth's fine group of children walked into the garden, which added to the agreeableness of the scene.

In her correspondence Mrs Delany left many accounts of her own beloved *'Paradisaical'* garden, Delville in Dublin, where one of her favourite features was a portico at the end of a terrace, 'prettily painted within and neatly finished without'. To decorate this, and presumably to light it at night, she made a chandelier decorated with shells, describing it in July 1744: 'My shell lustre I wrote you word I was about, was finished ten days ago and everybody liked it. Twas a *new whim* and shows the shells to great advantage . . . but the damp weather made the cement give and I have been obliged to bring it into the house . . .'

The garden umbrella was introduced in 1755 by Charles Over in his collection of designs entitled *Ornamental Architecture in the Gothic, Chinese and Modern Taste*: 'An umbrello seat after the Indian manner, being one of the

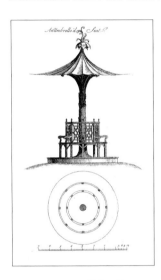

'An Umbrello'd Seat' by Charles Over. Although he described it as Indian, it is really more in the Chinese style.

most agreeable decorations yet known, from its affording shade when extended, and being on occasion easily contracted or removed.' Such umbrellas were still a novelty worth comment the next century. Prince Hermann von Pückler-Muskau, aged forty and newly divorced, visited England in 1826: a 'rogue, rover and rake' with a passion for landscape gardening and a mission to find a rich heiress to marry. In letters to his ex-wife he gives graphic accounts of his dazzling social life. After a visit to Lord and Lady Harcourt at St Leonard's Hill near Windsor in August 1827, he wrote in a letter: 'A most useful contrivance in this garden was a gigantic umbrella as large as a little tent, with an iron spike at the bottom to stick into the ground. You could thus establish yourself in any spot shaded from the sun.' By the 1920s the garden umbrella was a well-established piece of garden furniture with all manner of fringes and tilting mechanisms. It was, however, considered suburban, as is evident in a disparaging comment two architectural writers, Harry Batsford and Charles Fry, made in 1938 in *The English Cottage*, regretting the gutting of a Sussex Tudor cottage by the 'editress of a ladies' journal' for a weekend retreat which involved 'Sunday afternoons of actresses and popular novelists beneath striped umbrellas:

tea, talk and cocktails, with a glimpse of tortured half-timber through the rambler roses.'

Tents had many advantages as garden shelters. Early on they were perceived as Turkish ('such as sultans take when they go to war' was how the novelist Fanny Burney imagined their origins) and dotted around as incidental and fashionable structures in landscape gardens such as Painshill in Surrey and Stourhead in Wiltshire. Caroline Lybbe Powys considered that at Stourhead to be very pretty, describing it in her diary as 'of painted canvas, so remains up the whole year; the inside painted blue and white in mosaic'. However, she was more impressed with the radical garden tents that she saw on the Isle of Wight in 1792 when visiting Sandown Cottage, a summer cottage belonging to a Mr Wilkes, who called it the Villakin:

Detail from an advertisement in the May 1922 issue of *The Ideal Home* for a striped umbrella with valance costing 67s.

It commands an uncommon view of the sea and surrounding cliffs, very fine garden, in which is a menagerie. Strangers have leave to see the place by setting down their names in a book kept on purpose. The cottage only has a very few small rooms; but as Mr. Wilkes often entertains many families, he has erected in the gardens many of the fashionable canvas ones, fitted up in different manners and of large dimensions. One call'd the 'Pavilion,' another the 'Etruscan,' a third a dressing-room of Miss Wilkes, others as bedrooms, all very elegantly furnish'd, and very clever for summer (and the Isle of Wight, where it seems a robbery was never known), but to us who reside so much nearer to the vicinity of the Metropolis, the idea of being abroad in such open apartments strikes one with some rather small apprehensions.

The tent for shade and shelter from rain had a great future in the garden that was only just being realized. J.B. Papworth published a design for a typical Regency example, which he called a 'Venetian' tent, gaily striped in

Designs by J.B. Papworth for tented garden structures to be erected in summer.
Above: published by Ackermann in his *Repository of Arts* of 1822.
Below: the Venetian Tent from *Hints on Ornamental Gardening*, 1823.

red and white: 'a temporary retreat is a gratifying appendage to the house, and affords variety and healthfulness to the amusements of the day'. He stated that using this design it would only take half an hour to put the canvas on the ironwork frame and then decorative foliage could be tra.ined 'to embower the whole'. The marquee on the lawn, the staple of countless summer parties, fêtes and weddings, was thus born.

LATER PERMUTATIONS

As the nineteenth century progressed, the house and the garden became much more closely interconnected. There were French windows, opening out from ground-floor rooms, verandas, loggias, conservatories and flower gardens immediately surrounding the house. Use of the garden increased – a fact J.B. Papworth noted in *Hints on Ornamental Gardening* in 1823, applauding the fact that 'the fair sex were enabled to repossess their equal share of freedom, and were permitted the exercise of that brilliant intellect which is their inherent property', in that they could now easily use the garden for 'occasional reading or study' and the lawns and walks were not so remote and inaccessible that women were prevented from 'hourly enjoyment of both, and [could] certainly afford by this juncture a large proportion of healthful and pleasurable occupation'.

Ever-inventive Victorian manufacturers were alive to the possibility of turning a handsome profit from selling a welter of garden equipment to the burgeoning number of garden owners with money and time. Books and magazines offered advice, and machines and tools were supplied for every procedure. Garden seating alone was an area of almost limitless possibility. The influential arbiter on gardens J.C. Loudon declared in *The Suburban Gardener and Villa Companion* (1838):

> Seats are essential objects in all pleasure-grounds. In those of the most extensive and highly enriched description, where the main part of the intention is to display the wealth and taste of the owner, they may appear as Grecian temples, Gothic porches, Chinese pagodas, or other foreign or antique structures. In other grounds of less ambitious villas, plain unarchitectural buildings may be employed, or wooden structures, simply protecting the seat from the weather, may be resorted to.

Loudon was firmly of the view that in small gardens open and covered seats should be introduced with the greatest caution, and never as conspicuous features, 'because more than one, for the sake of being able to read or work in the open air, can seldom be requisite'. Among various novel items of garden furniture Loudon promoted were Chinese porcelain seats 'which will serve as ornaments as well as useful objects, [and] ought to be confined to the parapet wall of the terrace'. Jane Carlyle bought two of these 'little china barrel-shaped things' for her garden in the summer of 1857 and her husband Thomas was photographed perched on one (see page 23).

Victorian landscape gardeners, like those before them, loved to design pavilions, kiosks and summer houses in a range of styles, but with their generation's eye for comfort; 'these little buildings are very pleasant places for a quiet hour's reading, and the farther away from the house the greater the necessity for making them comfortable . . . A few panes of glass may prevent a fatal cold from draughts.' As ever in the garden the

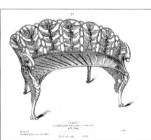

taste police were never far away: 'a thatched summer-house and a cut-stone mansion are incongruous; the 'Tower of the Winds' in Portland Cement will not agree with a cottage ornée, which by the way is generally an abomination' – at least these were the views of John Arthur Hughes, expressed in *Garden Architecture and Landscape Gardening* in 1866.

Cast-iron seating was a popular choice for garden furniture from the 1850s onwards: cold, heavy metal strangely transformed into hops, vines, water lilies, ivy, passion flowers and twigs to form benches, chairs and tables. Alternatives were available in Gothic (quatrefoil tracery), Elizabethan (strapwork motifs), Italian (arabesques and putti) or Moresque styles. Some garden writers believed that iron furniture

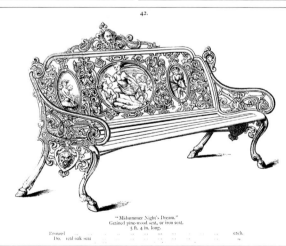

Designs from the Coalbrookdale Iron Company's catalogue of garden furniture, 1860s. Above: 'Passion Flower' and 'Laurel'. Below: 'Midsummer Night's Dream'.

91

had no place in the garden at all and that 'the association connected with iron and its manufacture' made it 'the reverse of rural', and these seats tended to be more popular in towns and suburbs. Such a bench is described as 'about as comfortable as a grid-iron' in Emily Eden's 1859 novel *The Semi-Detached House*; a fire in the kitchen flue fills the house with smoke and the elderly Aunt Sarah, the pregnant Blanche and her sister Aileen have to take refuge, armed with cushions and cloaks, in their 'wretched little asylum in the garden', which is half trellis and half earwigs, and they are forced to spend a wet afternoon on the hard seat. The Coalbrookdale Iron Company in Shropshire, principal manufacturer of iron garden furniture, commemorated the tercentenary of Shakespeare's birth by producing a bench named 'Midsummer Night's Dream', ornamented with a medallion bust of Shakespeare and relief plaques of Bottom, Oberon, Titiana and assorted fairies, the whole supported on furry asses' feet.

Stone seats in larger English gardens were inclined to be grand; a Victorian visitor to Chiswick House, for instance, the early-eighteenth-century Palladian villa and garden created by Lord Burlington, was awestruck by Burlington's classical stone benches and imagined them as 'the identical seats upon which the senators were reposing in majestic gravity and awful silence, when Brennus entered Rome'. But the trouble was that Britain was not Italy and, as the Edwardian garden designer Thomas Mawson noted, for eleven months of the year stone was cold and comfortless and even dangerous to health, a notion seconded by Gertrude Jekyll, who described stone as 'only good for the eye to repose on' and not, she implied, for the British bottom to sit on. Nevertheless Italian gardens were a source of inspiration for the cognoscenti at the turn of the century, so it is unsurprising to find that John P. White of Bedford offered real marble seats carved with scrolling foliage and lion's paw feet: the 'Lugano' cost the substantial sum of £42 10s. 0. The firm also sold Italian terracotta seats from Tuscany, made 'by a colony of artists, situated among the most glorious surroundings and far remote from any railway station. A great number made are reproductions from some of the finest work of old Italian masters, Verocchio, Michael Angelo and Donatello.'

HAMMOCKS AND LOUNGING ABOUT

Men have always been allowed to lie elegantly on the ground, the classic position for proclaiming your poetic sensibilities; such an attitude, head in hand, was that of the Elizabethan poet. It was also how Alfred Lord Tennyson remembered his friend Arthur Hallam in 'In Memoriam A.H.H.' (1849), lying in the shade in the garden:

> O bliss, when all in circle drawn
> About him, heart and ear were fed
> To hear him, as he lay and read
> The Tuscan poets on the lawn.

There came a point in the nineteenth century when it became possible for women, too, to relinquish stiff upright garden chairs and gently attain horizontality. The swing may have been the thin edge of the wedge. Rather surprisingly Jane Loudon, in the *Lady's Country Companion*, remarks that a swing is a very useful adjunct to the amusements of the country, as many grown-up people are as fond of swinging as children. If no trees were handy, Jane Loudon suggests what is in effect a swing seat – that garden feature later so beloved by early twentieth-century suburbanites: 'Two upright pieces of wood may be driven into the ground, with hooks or rings affixed to the upper part . . . a swing of this kind is generally furnished with a chair or boat, but is more fitted for some piece of enclosed ground.' She cites a garden hammock at the Duke of Devonshire's house at Chiswick being slung between two trees but intended for swinging.

By the 1880s hammocks had become a garden craze, rather than merely a practical sleeping arrangement for sailors. Increasingly elaborate, they included valances, covers and 'spreaders', a spreader being the rod which kept the hammock stretched wide at either end rather than enclosing the person as if they were an undignified sausage roll. Perhaps because of the daring horizontality they allowed the female figure, hammocks had a louche reputation, as is clear from a scene in Rhoda Broughton's 1886 novel *Doctor Cupid*. The unpleasantly fast Lady Betty demonstrates that she is unworthy of the hero John Talbot's love by leading the way on a hot Sunday afternoon to

where, beneath a great lime-tree only just out of flower, hangs the hammock, spread with wolf-skins, stand the wicker-chairs and tables, the iced drinks and the Sunday papers.

'Now we'll be happy!' says Betty, sitting down sideways on the hammock, and adroitly whisking her legs in after her. 'As soon as milady's back is turned, I will have a cigarette, and you shall talk me to sleep. By-the bye,' with a slight tinge of umbrage in her tone, 'your conversation of late has rather tended to produce that effect.'

'And what better effect could it produce?' asks John ironically. 'I sometimes wish that I could get some one to talk me to sleep for good and all!'

'How tiresome!' cries his fair one, not paying much heed to this lugubrious aspiration, and feeling in her pocket. 'I have left my cigarette-case in the house; go, like a good fellow, and get it for me. Ask Julie for it.'

He goes with the dull docility of a pack-horse or a performing poodle.

THE "USONA" HAMMOCK STAND AND AWNING.

A double hammock illustrated in W.B. Fordham & Son's catalogue 'Garden and Sporting Requisites for the Summer Season', 1909.

Fortunately for the heroine, the garden-loving Margaret, with whom John falls in love after helping her mow the lawn, he eventually tires of Lady Betty and 'his weary afternoons of hammock, scandal and cigarettes'.

Two years after this was written George Gissing included a hammock scene in his novel *A Life's Morning*. Beatrice Redwing, vegetarian and New Woman, enjoys the hammock in the garden of the Firs in Surrey. The hammock is no longer the refuge of the fast woman, but the heroine is unconventional. The hero, Wilfred Athel, and his father found Beatrice reclining in a hammock which had recently been suspended in a convenient spot. She had one hand beneath her head, the other held a large fan, with which she warded off stray flakes of sunlight falling between the leaves.

'Isn't this exquisite?' she cried. 'Let no one hint to me of stirring before lunch-time. I am going to enjoy absolute laziness.'

'I thought you would have preferred a gallop over the downs,' said Mr. Athel.

'Oh, we'll have that this afternoon; you may talk of it now and I shall relish it in anticipation.'

Her 'absolute laziness' in the hammock allows the hero to admire her physical form:

When Mrs. Rossall returned from the house with a magazine and a light shawl, the occupant of the hammock was already sound asleep. She threw the shawl with womanly skill and gentleness over the shapely body. When she had resumed her seat, she caught a glimpse of Wilfred at a little distance; her beckoned summons brought him near.

'Look,' she whispered, pointing to the hammock. 'When did you see a prettier picture?'

The young man gazed with a free smile, the expression of critical appreciativeness. The girl's beauty stirred in him no mood but that. She slept with complete calm of feature; the half-lights that came through the foliage made an exquisite pallor on her face, contrasting with the dark masses of her hair. Her bosom rose and fell in the softest sighing; her pure throat was like marble, and her just parted lips seemed to need a protector from the bees . . .

By the end of the century hammocks must have lost their mildly unsavoury reputation, since they appear in old photographs in the most sedate company. For the garden that lacked suitable trees from which to hang it, any number of patented arrangements with stands, telescopic hammock supports and automatic self-opening devices were available.

The somnolence of the late Victorian garden, with its increasingly comfortable chairs, is perfectly evoked by E.F. Benson in his novel *Dodo* (1894):

> This particular garden has always seemed to me the ideal of what a garden should be. It is made to sit in, to smoke in, to think in, to do nothing in. A wavy, irregular lawn forbids the possibility of tennis, or any game that implies exertion or skill, and it is the home of sweet smells, bright colour, and chuckling birds. There are long borders of mignonette, wallflowers and hollyhocks, and many old-fashioned flowers, which are going the way of all old fashions . . . If

A *Punch* cartoon of 1886 by George du Maurier features figures
luxuriating in a country house garden on various patterns of basket chair.

you had exploring tendencies in your nature, and had happened to find yourself, on the afternoon of which I propose to speak, in this delightful garden, you would sooner or later have wandered into a low-lying grassy basin, shut in on three sides by banks of bushy rose-trees. The faint, delicate smell of their pale fragrance would have led you there, or perhaps, the light trickling of a fountain, now nearly summer dry. Perhaps the exploring tendency would account for your discovery. There, lying in a basket-chair, with a half-read letter in her hand, and an accusing tennis racquet by her side, you would have found Edith Staines.

Following the original meaning of lounge as 'to be idle and do nothing', the earliest reclining chairs were 'lounges' and then became 'loungers'. The Victorian introduction of basket and wicker garden furniture provided squashier and softer seating; in *Gardens in the Making* the garden writer Walter Godfrey described these seats as 'instruments of idleness', to be bought into the garden whenever 'summer weather invites us to rest beneath the open sky'. Gertrude Jekyll agreed in *Gardens for Small Country Houses* that 'for sheer comfort there is no doubt that something of flimsy appearance made of canvas and a few sticks or of basket-work is best'. The Dryad company, which was set up in Leicester in 1907 with the worthy intention of building on local skills of working with willow and straw, specialized in large capacious garden chairs, and included one in their range unforgettably named 'Sluggard's Lure'. The model 'Miss Matty' was surely named for the character from Mrs Gaskell's *Cranford*, and intended for gentle gossiping. A 1936 article in *The Lady* described an 'amusing wicker bundler' that promised the possibility of lounging in pairs; the journalist ffrida Wolfe enthused about how it held two people very comfortably and had gay chintz-covered cushions and a fringed hood.

FURNISHING A GARDEN

Portable folding chairs were a great boon to sitting in the garden, suiting gardens of every size, as they were easy to move to catch sun or shade and to pack away in winter. A surge of patent applications from the 1880s onwards demonstrates the extent to which furniture makers had grasped their potential on land in the garden (as opposed to on deck at sea). Early specifications include head rests that converted into life buoys, and by 1899 S. W. Silver and W. Fletcher had devised a chair which incorporated baskets or receptacles for ladies' work or books that pivoted from the arm rests, or a box that 'could be swung round to form a book rest or table to support drinking-vessels, smoking-materials, Etc.' The straightforward wood and canvas deck chair – with no additions or modifications – seems to have appeared in January 1900. Its patentee, C.J. Wiseman, was the first to use the clever and simple device of the back strut of the 'folding and portable hammock chair' that fitted into ratchets, 'like a die in a matrix'. This clearly went a long way towards ensuring secure seating. For the heavyweight, there was the possible addition of an auxiliary weight-supporting attachment, a piece of extra fabric that could be adapted to form a carrying bag when the item was not in position on the chair. The difficulty of setting up a deck chair and nervousness about its stability were anxieties that the inventors and manufacturers attempted to quell. A.E. Rivers in 1911 patented a deck chair with metal hand grips to prevent fingers being trapped during folding and unfolding: the 'New Safety Hammock Chair', fitted with the 'Patent Holdfast Clutch'. A passage in Richmal Crompton's *Family Roundabout* explains the underlying problem:

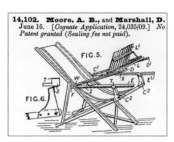

One of the many designs submitted to the Patent Office for folding garden chairs: this, filed in 1909 (but not granted), incorporated a detachable table and book rest.

> One Sunday afternoon in the July of 1920 Mrs. Fowler was sitting in her wicker chair under the lime tree at the end of the terrace. It was a shabby chair, with stray bits of wicker protruding from arms and legs, but it was comfortable and Mrs. Fowler preferred it to a deck-chair. She said that she always got entangled in deck-chairs when she tried to put them up herself, and, when they were finally put up by someone else, she never felt quite safe.

Furnishing the garden had become a serious subject. An article in *Ideal Home* for May 1922 commented: 'There is no reason why our gardens should not be as well furnished as our indoor apartments.' The summer of 1921 had evidently been a brilliant one, and such a summer carries with it a great inducement to live in the garden as much as possible; and a garden without furniture is useless for such a purpose. There are people who take all meals in the garden during good weather; some, indeed, who sleep outdoors on hot nights; and for all these purposes furniture is required – chairs of all kinds, settees, tables and quite a number of smaller pieces of furniture; as well as cushions, and, perhaps even a comfortable bed arrangement.

Page from Harrods' 1895 catalogue exhibiting garden furniture ranging from the solidly rustic to the light and adjustable.

For some, light Lloyd Loom garden furniture was the solution, a patented product of paper-covered wire 'as easy to clean as a main deck'; but solid sets of garden furniture made of Burmese teak were popular buys during the 1920s and 1930s, the boom bizarrely fuelled by the decommissioning of numbers of British warships and liners. This inspired recycling exercise led to companies such as Hughes Bolckow Shipbreaking Co. Ltd. of Blyth in Northumberland becoming manufacturers of garden furniture; 'From the Seven Seas to Your Garden' was their motto. Inspired perhaps by naval architecture, the furniture often cunningly interlocked in a space-saving fashion. The sets were named for admirals and ships such as Collingwood and *Thunderer*. It was perhaps superfluous for the manufacturers to point out that, having 'braved the battle and the breeze', the teak could be left out in all weathers. Shortly before the Second World War broke out, in 1935 the firm offered in its catalogue a seat with a sadly inappropriate motto: 'The glow of the dawn for glory, The hush of the night for peace, In the garden of Eve, says the story, God walks, and his smile brings release.'

Elizabeth Bowen analyses the nuances of the subject of sitting out in the garden in a scene from her novel *Friends and Relations*, published in 1931.

> The white afternoon, undisturbed by any wind or sunshine, undeepened personally by any hostility or attraction, hung gently, heavily over Batts. The large yellow stone house was quiet, with loud clocks. Rodney finished *The Observer* in the library, pressed the paper back into its folds and took it out to Colonel Studdart. He knew his father-in-law would have been glad of it sooner, but there were limits to hospitality. By this time, as it turned out, Colonel Studdart was asleep, his panama tipped over his eyes, in a wicker chaise-longue under the copper beech. Under the same maroon canopy another chaise-longue, empty, indicated an intention of Janet's. This quest of shade on a sunless day surprised Rodney, but Colonel Studdart's reasoning was faultless: you sat out only when it was hot, and when it was hot you sought a fine dark shadow. Colonel Studdart, to whom consciousness among all these cushions must have been pleasant, seemed sorry to have fallen asleep; a droop of incomplete resignation lengthened his chin.

Rodney is a countryman and fails to see the suburban attraction – as he sees it – of sitting out in the garden and doing nothing: 'he associated this fancy of Colonel Studdart's with pine-woods, bus-routes, the proximity of the neo-Tudor gable and a portable gramophone.'

Rodney disapproves in the manner of the much-quoted Kipling poem 'The Glory of the Garden':

> Our England is a garden and such gardens are not made
> By singing 'Oh how beautiful' and sitting in the shade,

which substantiates the perennial tension between gardeners and idle sitters. Ethelind Fearon in *The Reluctant Gardener* (1952) stoutly refuted Kipling as pernicious nonsense:

> . . . that's just exactly how gardens *are* made; the best and most personal and most peaceful gardens . . . And if you had some energetic friend hacking and hoeing away in them from morning to night . . . where would be the peace? There would be no peace at all and you would have to take refuge in the coal cellar.

Illustration by Alex Jardine
to the chapter in *The Reluctant Gardener*,
1952, entitled 'Something to Sit Under'.

5 A PLACE FOR EATING, DRINKING AND SMOKING

Eating out of doors in perfect weather is one of life's greatest pleasures, all the senses alive to the moment. That food tastes better outside is a remark often made, though it cannot logically be true. But certainly nothing can improve on wandering around a garden grazing, plums off the tree, peas off the vine, raspberries off the cane or gooseberries off the bush.

FRUIT

'What was *Paradise*? but a Garden and Orchard of trees and hearbs, full of pleasure? and nothing there but delights.' So wrote the Jacobean gardener William Lawson in *A New Orchard & Garden*. His near contemporary Andrew Marvell expresses the thought more lushly in 'The Garden':

> What wondrous life is this I lead!
> Ripe apples drop about my head;
> The luscious clusters of the vine
> Upon my mouth do crush their wine;
> The nectarine and curious peach
> Into my hands themselves do reach;
> Stumbling on melons as I pass,
> Insnared on flowers, I fall on grass.

In her novel *North and South* (1855) Mrs Gaskell's characters are much less abandoned about eating fruit in the garden, but the pleasure is still acute. At the end of an impromptu lunch in the Hales' cottage in the New Forest, Mr Hale proposes pears for dessert:

> 'There are a few brown beurrés against the south wall which are worth all foreign fruits and preserves. Run, Margaret, and gather some.'

Anonymous watercolour, *c*.1760, of two men drinking
under an arbour in a garden in Walthamstow.

'I propose that we adjourn into the garden, and eat them there,' said Mr. Lennox. 'Nothing is so delicious as to set one's teeth into the crisp, juicy fruit, warm and scented by the sun. The worst is, the wasps are impudent enough to dispute it with one, even at the very crisis and summit of enjoyment.' . . .

'I shall arm myself with a knife,' said Mr. Hale; 'the days of eating fruit so primitively as you describe are over with me. I must pare it and quarter it before I can enjoy it.'

Margaret made a plate for the pears out of a beet-root leaf, which threw up their brown gold colour admirably. Mr. Lennox looked more at her than at the pears; but her father, inclined to cull fastidiously the very zest and perfection of the hour he had stolen from his anxiety, chose daintily the ripest fruit, and sat down on the garden bench to enjoy it at leisure.

It was a garden full of ripe currants that entranced the poet Laurie Lee and his siblings on the day that the family moved into their cottage in the Slad Valley in Gloucestershire. There was nothing to eat but bread, and the fruit. 'The currants were in their prime, clusters of red, black, and yellow berries all tangled up with wild roses,' he wrote in *Cider with Rosie* (1959). 'Here was bounty the girls had never known before, and they darted squawking from bush to bush, clawing the fruit like sparrows.'

BANQUETS AND PICNICS

In the seventeenth century a garden banquet was not an elaborate meal but a delicious spread that included fruit, special sweetmeats and drinks. Banqueting houses were built for the purpose. The word banquet derives from the French *banque*, meaning a sitting bench or bank. Suitable recipes for these garden feasts were given by Gervase Markham in *Countrey Contentments, or The English Huswife* 'to the manner of Banquetting stuffe and conceited dishes, with other pretty and curious secrets necessary for the understanding of our English Housewife' with the unforgiving remark 'whosover is ignorant within, is lame, and but half of a compleat Housewife'.

His suggestions for suitable dishes include fresh cheese, spice cakes, quince cakes, marchpane, Banbury cake and jumbles – take 'whites of three eggs and beate them well, and then take a pound of fine wheat flower and sugar together finely siftd, and a few aniseeds well rubd and dried; then work together as stiff as you can work it, and so make them in what formes you please, and bake them in a soft overn upon white papers'. For drinking: sweet water – 'of the best kind, take a thousand damask roses, two good handful of lavender nops, a three pennyweight of mace, two ounces of cloves bruised, a quart of running water . . . distill it . . . and hang in the glass of water a graine or two of muske wrapt in a piece of sarcenet or fine cloth.'

In his *Survey of London* the antiquarian John Stow describes particular evenings when Londoners would eat out of doors. During the summer months of June and July bonfires were lit in the streets 'not only for rejoicing sake, but to cleanse the air . . . The wealthy citizens place bread and good drink upon the tables before their doors upon the vigil of the festival; but on the festival evening the same tables were more plentifully furnished with meat and drink, to which not only the neighbours but passengers were also invited to sit and partake, with great hospitality.'

John Aubrey describes the banqueting house built by Francis Bacon as being on an island in the middle of one of his ponds 'of Roman architecture, paved with black and white marble; covered with Cornish slatt, and neatly wainscotted'. Gervase Markham covers the question of open-air eating in *A Way to Get Wealth* and explains in his chapter on the subject of entertaining 'any great person, in any Parke, or other place of pleasure' that what was needed were 'arbours and Summer-bowers to feast, the fashion whereof is so common that every labourer can make them'. At Wimbledon House, the Cecil family's suburban retreat from London, there were circular green wooden banqueting houses with opposing doors opening out to different views on either side, perhaps not commonplace. The original Banqueting House at Whitehall Palace was canvas and wood hung with ivy, the roof painted with clouds and the outside walls to appear like rusticated stone.

In the eighteenth century meals in the garden tended to be light, delicious treats partaken in small confections of buildings or particular beauty spots, ideally accompanied by music. The eponymous heroine in *Pamela, or Virtue Rewarded* by Samuel Richardson (1741) has cakes and canary wine in a summer house. Henrietta Luxborough chose to eat syllabub on her birthday, which she ate under her venerable oak after a game of bowls, to the accompaniment of a soldier playing the German flute – what she termed *'des amusemens champetres'*. Mrs Delany wrote to her sister one June from Delville, her country house in Ireland:

> My garden is at present in the high glow of beauty, my cherries ripening, roses, Jessamine and pinks in full bloom, and the hay partly spread and partly in cocks, complete the rural scene. We have discovered a new break-fasting place under the shade of the nut-trees, impenetrable to the sun's rays, in the midst of a grove of elms, where we shall breakfast this morning; I have ordered cherries, strawberries, and nosegays to be laid on our breakfast-table, and have appointed a harper to be here to play to us during our repast, who is to be hid among the trees. Mrs. Hamilton is to breakfast with us, and is to be cunningly led to this place *and surprised.*

But sadly on that occasion Mrs Hamilton failed to arrive until twelve, so Mrs Delany had breakfast alone with her husband. Writing up one of the innumerable journeys that she and her husband Philip made from their house near Henley, Caroline Lybbe Powys described visiting a family near Chesterfield:

> One afternoon we were most agreeably entertained at Mrs. Bourn's, where we went to tea. Their gardens are charming, and as we drank tea in one of the buildings, the family being very musical and [having] charming voices, the young ladies sang, while the gentlemen accompanied on their German flutes. This little concert took up the heat of the day, after which we walk'd over the grounds. When in a little temple, on entering we laughed exceedingly at the rural politeness of our beaux; but as gentlemen of the army are always gallant, we were the less surprised at our elegant collation of fruit,

cakes, cream, placed in the most neat and rustic manner imaginable. This made us rather late home.

Tea at this period fitted into the delicious treat category. David Garrick in a letter to Hannah More describes how a friend from London had arrived from London and found him and his wife 'laughing over their tea under their walnut tree'. Oliver Goldsmith paints an equally elegiac picture in *The Vicar of Wakefield* when he describes Dr Primrose and his wife sitting peacefully in their garden. 'At a small distance from the house my predecessor had made a seat overshadowed by a hedge of hawthorn and honeysuckle. Here when the weather was fine and our labour soon finished we usually sat together to enjoy an extensive landscape in the calm of the evening. Here, too, we drank tea, which had become an occasional banquet.'

Rowlandson's early-nineteenth-century illustration of Goldsmith's 1766 text: Dr Primrose breakfasting outside while his daughters sing to him.

Of course, as always with social events, the whole scheme could misfire, as Horace Walpole's rather grumpy letter written during the summer of 1770 when he was fifty-three, testifies. He was at Stowe:

> The idea was really pretty, but, as my feelings have lost something of their romantic sensibility, I did not enjoy the entertainment

al fresco as much as I should have done twenty years ago . . . I could not help laughing as I surveyed our troop, which instead of tripping lightly to such an Arcadian entertainment, were hobbling down by the balustrades wrapped up in coats and great-coats, for fear of catching cold . . . we were none of us young enough for a pastoral. We supped in the grotto, which was proper to this climate as a sea-coal fire would be in the dog-days at Tivoli.

Humphry Repton noted with approval in *Sketches and Hints* that some great gardens such as at Longleat in Wiltshire were open to the public even for picnics: 'This magnificent park, so far from being kept locked up to exclude mankind from partaking of its scenery, is always open and parties are permitted to bring refreshments.' Engravings of the period show figures sitting around in the foreground looking out over the first Marquis of Bath's park to the great house. For the owners of such extensive landscape gardens a trip to a summer house could take on the nature of an expedition. One of the most enthusiastic was the Duke of Newcastle, who entertained at Claremont in Surrey in the mid-eighteenth century. He arranged picnics in his landscape garden, some on the island in the middle of his small lake and some in the Belvedere: 'My Lord and Lady Effingham, Mr. Vincent and his Lady of Stoak and six more dined at the Cottage, I gave them fruit & Ice Creams.' Instructions sent in a letter to his wife Henrietta to the Duchess for one picnic survive: 'I begg you would order hott Rolls for bread and butter, Ice Cream, and some cold Ham and Chickens, you will therefore order a Ham to be boiled for tomorrow for Cold, & some chickens to be roasted, we will have fruit and these things on the Island, lett Prevost make some Cherry water and some Leomonade [sic] in Ice.' He was vastly proud of his fruit and had six acres of walled garden planted with peaches, apples, plums, vines, gooseberries, mulberries, figs and apricots.

In stark contrast a much later, sadder and far more austere vision of a garden picnic is conjured up by the government's Holidays at Home campaign during the Second World War, which attempted to make a virtue of a necessity. The campaign was a bright idea that was also conveniently fuel saving. A 1944 leaflet from the Ministry of Food has suggestions which include sandwiches made with pilchard and cabbage spread, mock hamburgers cooked the night before (a little mince bulked out with potato and oatmeal) or coleslaw sandwiches (shredded cabbage in a 'very thin white sauce').

Ministry of Food advice on menus, illustrated with a rather sparse garden picnic.

PROPER MEALS

The Victorians introduced afternoon tea to fill the gap between lunch and an increasingly later dinner. Favoured by those at leisure during the day, primarily women and children, it was a comparatively informal meal; tea to drink was accompanied by muffins, sandwiches, cakes and biscuits, and since these involved little cutlery and one plate they were easily transported into the garden. Notwithstanding the simplicity, the occasion might be fraught. Francis Kilvert, who as a curate apparently had plenty of time for such gentle enjoyment, recorded a classic accident in his diary in June 1870: 'At lawn tea Charlotte Thomas emptied her cup of tea into her lap and then in getting up shot part of the contents of her lap out on to Mrs. Allen's dress.

Henry James describes the gentle atmosphere of eating outdoors in detail in *Portrait of a Lady* (1881):

> Under certain circumstances there are few hours in life more agreeable that the hour dedicated to the ceremony known as afternoon tea . . . The implements of the little feast had been disposed upon the lawn of an old English country-house, in what I should call the perfect middle of a splendid summer afternoon. Part of the afternoon had waned, but much of it was left, and what was left was of the finest and rarest quality. Real dusk would not arrive for many hours; but

the flood of summer light had begun to ebb, the air had grown mellow, the shadows were long upon the smooth dense turf. They lengthened slowly, however, and the scenes expressed that sense of leisure still to come which is perhaps the chief source of one's enjoyment at such an hour . . . The shadows on the perfect lawn were straight and angular; they were the shadows of an old man sitting in a deep wicker-chair near the low table on which the tea had been served, and of the two younger men strolling too and fro, in desultory talk, in front of him. The old man had his cup in his hand; it was

Proper tea, transported out into the garden: silver, crocheted cloth and laden cake stand, somewhere in England in the early years of the twentieth century.

an unusually large cup, of a different pattern from the rest of the set and painted in brilliant colours. He disposed of its contents with much circumspection, holding it for a long time close to his chin, with his face turned to the house . . . The great still oaks and beeches flung down a shade as dense as that of velvet curtains; and the place was furnished, like a room, with cushioned seats, with rich-coloured rugs, with the books and papers that lay upon the grass.

At the turn of the twentieth century the move towards greater informality coincided with the fervent belief in fresh air. Garden owners became ambitious for more than a simple garden tea and wanted to lunch and dine outside. Since Edwardian ideas of comfort and social standards still prevailed, garden designers and writers of the period give much space and thought to the provision of shelters, loggias, arbours and garden houses for the purpose. 'Modern Habits in Favour of Dining Out-of-Doors' trumpeted a feature on country houses in 1911. Its author, the garden designer H. Avray Tipping, continues: 'There is no better moment to enjoy the fresh air and garden outlook than at mealtimes, an arrangement that makes this possible and pleasant should receive due consideration. In our changeable climate it is impossible to feel security if that space is not roofed and

H.M. Bateman, master of scenes of social embarrassment, suggests that dining outside on a hot summer evening has its disadvantages, 1913.

sheltered from driving winds.' He consolidates his argument for a roofed garden space by relating his experiences of breakfasting outside. 'I remember suffering frequent humiliation when the terrace where I used to breakfast lacked such a contrivance. I would over-rule my servant's strong objection to laying the breakfast there when the sky threatened, and often enough, by the time I sat myself down, a shower or a drizzle would set in. Even if, to save my dignity, I was prepared to face the elements, the salt was not, and the effect was disastrous on the cutlery. So I had to ring the bell, confess my error of judgment and beg that everything might be removed hurriedly indoors.' Using personal experience of rebellious household staff, let alone damp salt and cloudy silver, Avray Tipping stresses the importance of putting the outside dining room close to the kitchen quarters, pointing out that there would be 'persistent attempts to confine them [meals] to the dining room' if not. 'For there is no doubt that the perfection of open-air dining is to have nothing overhead between you and the sky. The fading of the daylight, the lighting up of the heavens, but shortly joined by myriad companions as night gains the ascendancy . . .'

The idea was catching on and Heal's catalogue for 1921, 'Summer Life in the Garden', pointed out that small gardens or even the balconies of London flats could be equipped with garden furniture ready for the right moment to indulge in the 'pure enjoyment' of a meal outside. 'Patio Living at Heal's' was the title of a special summer exhibition of furnishings held in 1934 by the influential Tottenham Court Road shop. The patio was a new labour-saving type of garden eminently suited to the increasingly small garden plot and the interwar economy with gardeners in short supply. In her history *The Pleasure Garden* the journalist Anne Scott-James saw the subsequent popularity of the patio as the result of the 1970s boom in foreign package holidays: they were an imitation of life seen in Spain and Italy, where eating outside was the norm.

Poster by Betty Cooke for Heal's 1938 Garden Furniture Exhibition, illustrating what appear to be the latest tubular metal loungers.

> A patio – the word of course is Spanish – is estate-agent's language for a backyard, and there is something inspiring in the high-sounding name. For while it is all too easy to allow a backyard to become a sordid site for naked dustbins, it is impossible to neglect a patio. Here, in the heart of his home, the owner re-lives the holidays he has spent in southern Europe; here he paves and plants in the Mediterranean manner; here he quaffs *vin rosé* and serves *scampi provençale*.

The vision has persisted happily into the twenty-first century, though the patio may now be a timber-slatted deck and the food served from a pottery chiminea, more normally found in the possession of a Mexican peasant. In lieu of warm Mediterranean evenings, the patio heater has appeared.

DRINKS IN THE GARDEN

While the ideal tea in the garden traditionally happened on a soft lawn in the shade of a large leafy tree, real drinking in the twentieth century tended to have a different focus. The venue was more likely to be a hard-edged patio, a terrace or beside a swimming pool – all thought perfect for a drink before lunch or dinner. A scene Agatha Christie set for her novel *The Hollow* (1946) has Hercule Poirot being led by a butler through the French windows, across the slope of the lawn, past a rockery to 'a small pavilion by the swimming pool where Sir Harry and Lady Angkatell are in the habit of having cocktails and sherry before lunch' (and where of course a body is found shot). The pavilion is furnished with a painted iron table, comfortable settees, wicker chairs and 'gay native rugs'. In John Betjeman's poem 'The Subaltern's Love Song' the young officer and Miss Joan Hunter Dunn have a strong drink on the veranda after 'the strenuous singles, played after tea':

'Cocktails à la Mode. A Cocktail Party in the Very Best Manner of the Period': one of Gilbert Rumbold's decorations to *The Savoy Cocktail Book*, 1930.

Her father's euonymus shines as we walk
And swing past the summer-house buried in talk,
And cool the verandah that welcomes us in
To the six o'clock news and a lime juice and gin.

Cocktail parties became popular in the 1920s and 1930s and were easily thrown in a garden, it being a good place to carelessly stub out cigarettes and spill drinks without repercussion. In *Down the Garden Path* (1932) Beverley Nichols gave a sour description of drinking in town gardens during this period, deriding 'pools and cupids and cats, and very crazy pavements, and seats that are scrubbed, on rare summer evenings by sulky butlers. Tubs of startled scarlet geraniums, that have been popped into place a few hours before a cocktail party . . . Women in satin cloaks, drifting about on roof gardens, wondering if the clipped box standard affords sufficient concealment to enable them to make pretty faces at some other woman's man.'

SMOKING

Banishing the smoker from the house is not new: smoking was often enjoyed in gardens, from the old man enjoying his churchwarden pipe at the porch of his cottage to the Victorian gentleman in evening dress patrolling the terrace after dinner, while puffing at a cigar. Smoking was an accepted recreation for Victorian bachelors but there was a view that it should be given up after marriage: instead of lurking in the smoking room, lying around on a divan in a fez or retiring to the garden, husbands should join their wives in the familial sitting room.

William Cowper used a summer house in his neighbour's garden for both writing and smoking. It had been built during the early eighteenth century by an apothecary called Thomas Aspray specifically for the purpose of smoking. Cowper smoked there with his friends the Reverend John Newton and the Reverend William Bull. Bull rode over every week from nearby Newport Pagnell and stored his pipes and tobacco under the floorboards. Cowper also used to smoke in his greenhouse, a habit generally encouraged in gardening books as a good way to destroy pests. In a letter to Bull dated June 1783 he wrote:

A men's fashion plate for 1841 has them gathering around a garden bench to smoke cigars.

I hear nothing but the pattering of a fine shower and the sound of distant thunder, [it] wants only the fumes of your pipe to make it perfectly delightful. Tobacco was not known in the Golden Age. So much the worse for the Golden Age. This age of Iron and Lead would be insupportable without it, and therefore we may reasonably suppose that the Happiness of those better days would have much improved by the Use of it.

Thomas Carlyle was a smoker from the age of eleven and described tobacco as 'one of the divinest benefits that has ever come to the human race, arriving as compensation and consolation at any time when social, political, religious anarchy and every imaginable plague made earth unspeakably miserable.' Shortly after moving to 5 Cheyne Row, Chelsea, in 1834, he wrote to his mother saying what a perfect place the garden was to smoke his morning and evening pipes, which he did wearing his much-favoured long plaid dressing gown and wide straw hat. The garden was bounded with old walls and Carlyle apparently tucked spare clay pipes in gaps between the bricks for use at odd moments, sometimes smoking outside at night when he was unable to sleep.

Illustration from a Boulton & Paul advertisement for a summerhouse that exhorts clients to 'Make the Most of the Long Evenings', suggesting that 'in its pleasant interior you can sit and smoke and do what circumstance or the mood dictates'.

A glance through the patents submitted for garden furniture during the late nineteenth century shows that furniture-making companies saw smoking in the garden as a commercial opportunity. In 1899 Messrs. S.W. Silver and W. Fletcher patented a portable folding chair with boxes pivoted to the arms. These could contain pipes and tobacco and the cover could support drinking vessels and smoking materials; in addition there were attachments with holes for pipes and glasses. In the 1920s Dryad produced garden furniture woven from willow and straw with drinkers and smokers in mind: 'Abundance'and 'Pilgrim's Quest' were models with arm attachments for ashtray and pipes, while a set incorporating a drinks table was termed 'Lotus Eater'.

In Virginia Woolf's wartime novel *Between the Acts* the assembled company drink coffee and smoke cigarettes after lunch in the garden, and look out at the view:

> 'That's what makes the view so sad,' said Mrs Swithin, lowering herself into the deck-chair which Giles had brought her. 'And so beautiful. It'll be there,' she nodded at the strip of gauze laid upon the distant fields, 'when we're not.'
>
> Giles nicked his chair into position with a jerk. Thus only could he show his irritation, his rage with old fogies who sat and look at views over coffee and cream when the whole of Europe – over there – was bristling like . . . He had no command of metaphor. Only the ineffective word 'hedgehog' illustrated his vision of Europe, bristling with guns, poised with planes.

The scene ends with the smoker's gesture: '. . . William Dodge added, burying the end of his cigarette in a grave between two stones.'

BARBECUES

The barbecue arrived in the British back garden in the mid-1950s, an import from hotter and sunnier North America and Australia. Early barbecues were improvisations: *Woman's Own* for July 1958 suggested building a barbecue yourself with two layers of household bricks and a metal grill, which could be portable – since you never knew when the wind might change – if constructed on a sheet of metal. 'A footscraper makes an ideal griddle on which to cook the food,'proposed John Brookes in *Room*

Outside in 1969, and he also pointed out that barbecues were invaluable for burning rubbish. Trend-conscious Wedgwood produced a range of china called 'Barbecue' in the mid-fifties, decorated with barbecue-type food implements such as salad servers, pepper grinders and trivets, but with no clear image of the barbecue itself. *Barbecues,* a Penguin handbook published in 1977, claimed on its back cover that food cooked on a barbecue will 'bring a whiff of the exotic into your own back garden'. The British needed educating in the new art: 'Learn how to build them, how to cook with them and how to exploit them fully, using the recipes provided – sauces and marinades, barbecued honey pineapple, steak kebabs or barbecued lobster . . .' The author, James F. Marks, saw their popularity as an extension of hippy values – 'a consumer society eager to switch from armaments to the hibachi', showing a keenness to get 'back to the land' or, if necessary, the suburban back garden. During the 1970s and 1980s television soaps imported from Australia and the States, such as *Neighbours* and *Dallas*, possibly helped show the British how to hang around burning meat in the back garden with a beer in hand. After 1976 the advent of the battery-powered stereo machine, then known to many as a boombox, threw music into the smoky haze, thus creating a much louder type of eating in the garden.

A *Punch* cover for July 1964 parodies the British rain-soaked barbecue: the cook is frantically opening a tin in the kitchen.

6 A PLACE FOR LOVE, FLIRTATION AND UNWANTED ADVANCES

Social forms and manners can be relaxed out in the garden, away from the formality and bustle of the house. Gardens make for perfect trysting places, away from the inquisitive eyes of chaperones, siblings, parents or rivals. In addition their natural beauty provides scenic and romantic backdrops against which to further a suit.

An opportunistic medieval lover finding his maiden
in the garden: woodcut of 1460.

BOWERS, ARBOURS AND MAZES

The rose, a symbol of Venus, was, and still is, associated with love. Appropriately Venus was also the ancient Roman goddess associated with the garden. One of the most popular medieval tales was the *Roman de la*

Rose, a French allegorical romance written in the thirteenth century and translated into English, in part by Chaucer, as *The Romaunt of the Rose*. The setting is an enclosed garden and in it the narrator, the Dreamer, is pierced with an arrow by Cupid, and so becomes the Lover. Sequences include him being invited into the garden by the beautiful Idleness, a 'rich and puissant woman' with nothing else to think about except what clothes and jewels to wear and how to arrange her hair. She invites the Lover to spend time with her friend Mirth, who is holding court out on the grass 'in care-spurned ease for full enjoyment of life's glad gifts'. There follows an invitation to dance from the beautiful Courtesy, at the end of which the Dreamer wanders around and sees, in the words of a nineteenth-century adaptation:

> Beneath the burgeoning mulberry trees,
> Laurels, lithe hazels, and dark pines,
> Throughout the garden's far confines.
> And when the swaying dance was ended,
> And, arms entwined, the partners wended
> To seek soft couches, 'neath the shade
> That long lawn-kissing branches made.

A 1481 woodcut illustrating the *Roman de la Rose*: the lover enters the garden and plucks a rose.

The Lover reaches for a rosebud that represents his love. Since then gardens, lovers and roses have been firmly entwined as a romantic vision. When Tennyson's Victorian lover, waiting alone at the garden gate, calls for Maud to 'Come into the garden' he too has a dialogue with a rose:

> I said to the rose, 'The brief night goes
> In babble and revel and wine.'
> O young lord-lover, what sighs are those,
> For one that will never be thine?
> 'But mine, but mine' so I sware to the rose
> 'For ever and ever, mine.'

One of the most enduring and most extreme examples of the garden as a context for love occurs in the legend of Rosamund's Bower. The truth was less romantic but the myth is a compelling tale and good source material for later literary endeavours. The story is that Henry II set up his mistress, Rosamund Clifford, in a bower in the garden of Woodstock Palace, near Oxford, and then surrounded both with a labyrinthine maze.

Dutch sixteenth-century engraving of a garden maze; winged Cupid points the way forward.

When Henry's wife, Eleanor of Aquitaine, called unexpectedly she noticed a thread hanging on Henry's spur and, suspicious, she proceeded, in true fairy-tale fashion, to follow the thread to its source to find Rosamund quietly stitching in her bower. Eleanor then either stabbed Rosamund or poisoned her. In truth evidence suggests that the bower was quite a substantial house with a chapel, cloister, kitchen and wine cellar and some fine water pools stocked with fish. Rosamund ended her life in the nunnery at Godstow, to which she was admitted in 1176. The Tudor poets Thomas Delaney in the *Ballad of Fair Rosamund* and Samuel Daniel in *Complaynt of Fair Rosamond* both turned the legend into poems — which may explain the presence of a maze, since it was a favourite feature of the period. Daniel envisioned Henry's garden at Woodstock as having

. . . intricate innumerable ways
With such confused errours, so beguiled
Th'unguided Entrers, with uncertaine strayes,
And doubtful turnings, kept them in delayes;
With bootless labor leading them about,
Able to finde no way, nor in, nor out.

Within the closed bosome of which frame,
That serv'd a Centre to that goodly Round,
Were lodgings, with a Garden to the same,
With sweetest flowers that ev'r adorn'd the ground,
And all the pleasures that delight hath found,
T'entertaine the sense of wanton eies;
Fuell of Love, from when lusts flames arise.

Mazes are perfect for the amorous pursuits of running, hiding, catching and getting lost, but being highly laborious to grow were rare. Simpler 'privy-playing places' were arbours, sheltered and secluded spots of interwoven plants and branches. Thomas Watson describes one where he spied his love in a poem 'Tears of Fancie' (1593):

I saw the object of my pining thought
Within a garden of sweete nature's placing,
Wherein an arbour, artificial wroughte,
By workeman's wondrous skill the garden gracing . . .

Thomas Hill carefully explains how to create an artificially wrought arbour in his *Gardener's Labyrinth* of 1577 (illustrated on page 76): 'the herber in a Garden may bee framed with Juniper poles, or the Willowe, eyter to stretch, or be bound together with Osyers, after a square forme, or in arch manner winded, that the braunches of the Vine, Melone, or Cucumbre, running and spreading all over, might so shadowe and keepe both the heate and Sunne from the walkers and sitters thereunder.'

DANGEROUS PLACES

Incidental garden buildings are central to garden flirtations. In *The Anatomie of Abuses* (1583) the godly and zealous writer Philip Stubbes was hostile to almost everything lighthearted in contemporary Elizabethan society, including May Day, public dancing, wakes and football, and he saved a few judgmental lines for garden houses: 'In the fields and suburbs of the cities, they have gardens either palled or walled round about very high, with their harbers and bowers fit for the purpose. And least they might be espied in these open places, they have their banqueting houses with galleries, turrets, and what not, therein sumptuously erected; wherein they may (and doubtless do) many of them play the filthy persons . . .'

Samuel Pepys's London garden became a place of temptation in the 'mighty hot' days of the summer of 1666, when in the cool of the night he began singing outside in the company of his wife and their maid Mercer. He first mentions this in his diary on 19 June: 'Thence home, and at my business till late at night, then with my wife into the garden and there sang with Mercer, whom I feel myself begin to love too much by handling of her breasts in a' morning when she dresses me, they being the finest that ever I saw in my life, that is the truth of it.' He repeats the performance the next night, after which his wife (unsurprisingly perhaps) has a row with the delectable Mercer, who is

Clarissa, another of Samuel Richardson's heroines, in a flutter: Robert Lovelace preparing to abduct Clarissa Harlowe, painted by Francis Hayman, 1753–4. 'A panic next to fainting seized me when I saw him. My heart seemed convulsed . . .'

temporarily banished. But she is back by the evening of the 26th, when Pepys stays in his office till his eyes are sore and 'then into the garden, then my wife and Mercer and my Lady Pen and her daughter with us, and here we sung in the darke very finely half an houre'. Mercer sings a song called 'Helpe, helpe' very finely, he reports on another evening. At the very end of July Mrs Pepys loses patience, and he comes home to sing and 'find my wife plainly dissatisfied with me, that I can spend so much time with Mercer, teaching her to sing, and could never take the pains with her'.

With temples, gazebos, pavilions, grottoes and hermitages in styles rustic, Turkish, chinoiserie, Rococo or classical among the most fashionable of garden features, the Georgian garden offered much scope for secluded assignations. Owners of extensive landscape gardens might employ their stonemasons to create a miniature Pantheon, as Henry Hoare did at Stourhead; and there were plenty of simpler alternatives that could be picked from the pages of inexpensive pattern books such as William Pain's *The Builder's Companion and Workman's General Assistant* and quickly knocked up by a carpenter. And although the purpose of these buildings was to take tea in, to walk to, to shelter in or to provide a charming view, they lent themselves to other uses; indeed such a feature was exactly the sort of spot dreaded by poor Pamela, Samuel Richardson's heroine:

A hAPPY CHRISTMAS.

A soldier presses his suit on the housemaid as they sit on a garden bench – a surprising subject for a Christmas card, *c*.1890.

My master just now sent me down to take a walk with him in the garden; but I like him not at all, nor his ways; for he would have his arm about my waist, and said abundance of fond things, enough to make me proud, if his design had not been apparent. After walking about, he led me into a little alcove, on the farthest part of the garden; and really made me afraid of myself; for he began to be very teasing, and made me sit on his knee.

Fanny Burney puts her heroine in *Evelina* in much the same predicament in a Clifton town garden. Evelina is sitting in an arbour worrying about her future when she is interrupted by the arrival of Sir Clement Willoughby, who prevents her from leaving:

'Stop, stop,' cried he, 'loveliest and most beloved of women, stop and hear me!' . . .

I then rose, and was going, but he flung himself at my feet to prevent me, exclaiming, in a most passionate manner,' Good God! Miss Anville, what do you say? Is it, can it be possible, that so unmoved, that with such petrifying indifference, you can tear from me even the remotest hope!'

'I know not, Sir,' said I, endeavouring to disengage myself from him, 'what hope you mean, but I am sure that I never intended to give you any.'

'You distract me!' cried he, 'I cannot endure such scorn; – I beseech you to have some moderation in your cruelty, lest you make me desperate: – O fairest inexorable! Loveliest tyrant! – say, tell me, at least, that you pity me!'

Just then, who should come into sight, as if intending to pass by the arbour, but Lord Orville! Good Heaven, how did I start!

And he, the moment he saw me turned pale was hastily retiring: – but I called out 'Lord Orville! Sir Clement, release me, – let go my hand!'

Sir Clement, in some confusion, suddenly rose, but still grasped my hand. Lord Orville, who had turned back, was again walking away: but still struggling to disengage myself, I called out, 'Pray, pray, my Lord, don't go! Sir Clement I *insist* upon your releasing me!'

Lord Orville then, hastily approaching us, said, with great spirit, 'Sir Clement, you cannot wish to detain Miss Anville by force!'

'Neither, my Lord,' cried Sir Clement proudly, 'do I request the honour of your Lordship's interference.'

However, he let go my hand, and I immediately ran into the house.

William Shenstone at The Leasowes appeared quite blatant with his naming of the 'Assignation Seat', which he placed at the bottom of a Lover's Walk, 'its bounds so well concealed'. His friend and neighbour Lady Luxborough, who was separated from her husband and had a dubious reputation, wrote a curious letter to Shenstone in August 1749, which sheds a different and frivolous light on hermitages, normally associated with the idea of solitary meditation:

Mr Hall came yesterday in the evening to kiss your hands, but found Outing and me lamenting your absence; one seated on the turf, the other on a stone at the Hermit's door, who has acquired a new bed, which may hold not only you, if your colic should oblige you to lie down, but also all the agreeable company I hope to see with you. It is the Bed of Ware, the vulgar say, our friend Outing says it is only a sociable bed for two hermits and two hermitesses.

Horace Walpole described her as 'a high-coloured black woman . . . [who] corresponded with the small poets of the time, but as there was no Theseus amongst them, it was said that like Ariadne she had consoled herself with Bacchus'.

Walpole was presumably being catty about Henrietta Luxborough's drinking habits, but Bacchus and Venus were linked in a well-known quotation from the Roman comic dramatist Terence to the effect that without the stimulus of wine and feasting, love grows cold (*Sine Baccho et Cerere friget Venus*), and sculptures of both gods were commonly found as garden ornaments. Copies of the ancient Hellenistic statue known as the

One of several drawings by Thomas Rowlandson on the subject of lusty gardeners, *c.*1800.
The gardener falls to his knees with a bunch of flowers; the lady's dog
is no protection against an unwanted advance.

Medici Venus – which Edward Gibbon described as 'the most voluptuous sensation that my eye has ever experienced'– were particularly popular and were often placed as a centrepiece of a garden temple. Among the many garden decorations built by Lord Cobham at Stowe in Buckinghamshire, one of the most famous and visited gardens of the eighteenth century, was a Temple of Venus. The interior was frescoed with a scene from Spenser's *The Faerie Queen* where Malbecco spies on his unfaithful wife as she joins a band of satyrs in the forest. The atmosphere was clearly intended to be suggestive, and disapproving contemporary descriptions by the Reverend William Gilpin tell of 'luxurious couches' suggesting 'the loosest ideas'. A poem inscribed in Lord Jersey's Temple of Venus at Middleton Stoney had a warning to visitors, which may have inspired nervousness in some women:

> Whoe'er thou art, whom chance ordains to rove,
> A youthful stranger to this fatal grove.
> Oh, if thy breast can feel too soft a flame,
> And with thee wanders some unguarded dame,
> Fly, fly the place – each object thro' the shade
> Persuades to love . . .

More overtly erotic were the garden features created by the notorious Georgian rake Sir Francis Dashwood at West Wycombe. His Temple of Venus was placed on a mound into which was burrowed a rather gynaecological hole. In front of this Dashwood was advised by his friend Lord Bute to erect a Paphian column to augment a number of erotic statues placed on top of the mount. Reputedly he also had breast-shaped earthworks formed, which he surmounted with a planting of red flowers, and from the middle of these spouted fountains. Strategically below was triangular shrubbery also capable of gushing water.

UNDER TREES AND INTO SHRUBBERIES

Passion and a proposal in the garden as depicted by J.E. Millais in a pen-and-ink drawing entitled *Accepted*, 1853.

Anywhere in the garden would do for a romantic interlude, given fine summer weather or a moonlit night. Victorian novelists, taking their cue from real life, favoured placing girls in the shade of a tree, preferably scented. Charles Dickens makes David Copperfield see the angelic Dora 'sitting under a lilac tree upon a beautiful morning among the butterflies, in a white chip bonnet and a dress of celestial blue'. In *The White Rose* G. Whyte Melville places his heroine Nora 'in a white dress beneath the drooping lime-tree that gleamed and quivered in the sunbeams, alive with the hum of insects, heavy with its wealth of summer fragrance, and raining its shower of blossoms with every breath that whispered through its leaves'.

A seat encircling the trunk of a horse chestnut tree is where Edward Rochester proposes to Jane Eyre. Jane is wandering around the garden at Thornfield Hall on Midsummer's Eve when she scents, among the sweet briar and southernwood, jasmine, pink and rose, the 'warning fragrance' of Mr Rochester's after-dinner cigar. Jane tries to escape him, but he becomes aware of her presence and persuades her that 'on so lovely a night it is a shame to sit in the house, and surely no one can wish to go to bed while sunset is thus meeting with moonrise'.

> I did not like to walk at this hour alone with Mr. Rochester in the shadowy orchard; but I could not find a reason to allege for leaving him. I followed with lagging step, and thoughts busily bent on discovering a means of extrication; but he himself looked so composed and so grave also, I became ashamed of feeling any confusion: the evil – if evil existent or prospective there was – seemed to lie with me only; his mind was unconscious and quiet.

After the proposal – 'You, Jane, I must have you for my own – entirely my own. Will you be mine? Say yes, quickly' – which Jane, not knowing that Rochester already has a wife, accepts, Charlotte Brontë continues:

> But what had befallen the night? The moon was not yet set, and we were all in shadow: I could scarcely see my master's face, near as I was. And what ailed the chestnut tree? It writhed and groaned; while wind roared in the laurel walk, and came sweeping over us.
>
> 'We must go in,' said Mr. Rochester: 'the weather changes. I could have sat with thee till morning, Jane.'
>
> 'And so,' thought I, 'could I with you.' I should have said so, perhaps, but a livid vivid spark leapt out of a cloud at which I was looking, and there was a crack, a crash, and a close rattling peal; and I only thought of hiding my dazzled eyes against Mr. Rochester's shoulder.

That night the horse chestnut tree is struck by lightning and half of it split away.

The heroine of Benjamin Disraeli's lusciously florid novel *Henrietta Temple* is first spotted by the hero, Ferdinand Armine, under a cedar tree. Later it is in the summer twilight of the garden at Ducie Bower in Northamptonshire that he declares his passionate, though highly inconvenient, love. Henrietta's father has fortuitously been called away to Scotland, leaving Henrietta on her own.

> Full of hope, and joy, and confidence, he took her in his arms, sealed her cold lips with a burning kiss, and vowed to her his eternal and almighty love!
>
> He bore her to an old stone bench placed on the terrace. Still she was silent; but her hand clasped his, and her head rested on her bosom. The gleaming moon now glittered, the hills and woods were silvered by its beam, and the far meads were bathed with its clear, fair light. Not a single cloud curtained the splendour of the stars. What a rapturous soul was Ferdinand Armine's as he sat that

night on the old bench, on Ducie Terrace, shrouding from the rising breeze the trembling form of Henrietta Temple! And yet it was not the cold that made her shiver.

New opportunities for subterfuge appeared with the introduction of the shrubbery as a garden feature, replacing as it did linear terraces and walks with paths winding around choice specimens of laurel, azalea and rhododendron. Loudon explains in *The Suburban Gardener & Villa Companion* that even in a small garden the walks could be planned to give the visitor ever-changing small vistas. The art of planting a shrubbery involved 'concealment' of the walks themselves and he points out that this could be achieved by creating artificial undulations in even the smallest gardens, and increasing the number of walks by criss-crossing them with grotto-like tunnels and with bridges. It is easy to imagine that the chains of shrubs Loudon recommended quickly grew into dense thickets that were perfect for a couple to duck out of sight

Humphry Repton's 1816 design for a pavilion in the garden of a gothic mansion, depicting it in atmospheric moonlight and as easily accessible from the house.

behind. In *Hard Cash*, a novel with some testing scenes in a lunatic asylum written by Charles Reade in 1863, the seventeen-year-old schoolgirl Julia Dobbs is taken into the garden by a 'precocious boy, rather a flirt', the undergraduate Alfred Hardie. Julia's mother looks anxiously through the upstairs window of Albion Villa:

And the more she looked the more uneasy she grew.
The head, the hand, the whole body of a sensitive young woman

walking beside him betray her heart to experienced eyes watching unseen . . . Mrs. Dodd's first impulse was that of leopardesses, lionesses, hens, and all mothers in nature; to dart from her ambush and protect her young . . .

They entered the shrubbery.

To Mrs. Dodd's surprise and dismay they did not come out this side so quickly. She darted her eye into the plantation; and lo! Alfred had seized the fatal opportunity foliage offers, even when thinnish; he held Julia's hand, and was pleading eagerly for something she seemed not disposed to grant; for she turned away and made an effort to leave him. But Mrs. Dodd, standing there quivering with maternal anxiety, and hot with shame, could not but doubt the sincerity of that graceful resistance. She ceased even to doubt, when she saw her daughter's opposition ending in his getting hold of two hands instead of one, and devouring them with kisses.

Gwen Raverat's drawing of herself as a child in the role of 'the conscientious chaperon' during the 1890s.

The shrubbery is also the spot where Lily Dale and Adolphus Crosbie habitually say goodnight to one another in *The Small House at Allington* by Anthony Trollope. 'As he parted with her for the night on her own side of the little bridge which led from one garden to the other, he put his arm round her to embrace her and kiss her, as he had often done at that spot. It had become a habit with them to say their evening farewells there, and the secluded little nook amongst the shrubs was inexpressibly dear to Lily.'

MOONLIGHT AND ROSE GARDENS

The garden was traditionally a place to escape a chaperone; few of the spinster aunts traditionally assigned the role were happy to spend hours in draughty secluded corners of the garden. In her memoir *Period Piece*, describing an upbringing in middle-class academic Cambridge at the end of the nineteenth century, the artist Gwen Raverat describes and illustrates the 'discouraging chaperon' role:

There was one profession to which I was very early apprenticed: that of being chaperon to courting couples. My mother often had friends and younger sisters staying with her: they were charming people; sociable and foreign enough, being American, to be very attractive, and the chief excitement of her early life was the constant expectation that some of the Gentlemen, who were supposed to be 'very devoted' to them, would propose.

Chaperones were consigned to history by the time Aldous Huxley wrote *Crome Yellow*, published in 1921. The modern swimming pool is the scene of correspondingly twentieth-century casual behaviour. The young among the house party rush out into the garden after dinner and go down to the pool in the dark:

They walked along by the side of the pool, interlaced. Mary was too short for him to be able, with any comfort, to lay his head on her shoulder. He rubbed his cheek, caressed and caressing, against the thick, sleek mass of her hair. In a little while he began to sing again; the night trembled amorously to the sound of his voice. When he had finished he kissed her. Anne or Mary: Mary or Anne. It didn't seem to make much difference which it was. There were difference in detail, of course; but the general effect was the same; and, after all, the general effect was the important thing.

The young man, Ivor, and Mary later make love on the roof of the house.

P.G. Wodehouse's novels and stories bring the characteristic features of an Edwardian garden into full play. In *Crime Wave at Blandings* Lord Emsworth's sister, Lady Constance, bemoans the fact that their niece Jane has fallen in love with penniless and jobless George Abercrombie:

'I went down to the lake, and there discovered her with a young man in a tweed coat and flannel knickerbockers. They were kissing one another in the summerhouse.'

Lord Emsworth clicked his tongue.

'Ought to have been out in the sunshine,' he said disapprovingly.

But the rose garden was more obviously romantic and with easy access to red roses may have gradually taken over from the claustrophobic shrubbery as a favoured place of assignation. The Victorians grew roses in specially defined areas – usually geometric beds bounded by pergolas of climbers – and by the early twentieth century few self-respecting garden-owners lacked a rose garden. Such a setting enhanced the attractions of the fairer sex, as James Belford in Wodehouse's short story 'Pig Hoo-o-o-o-ey' found.

> 'How well I remember that rose garden,' said James Belford, sighing slightly and helping himself to Brussel sprouts. 'It was there that Angela and I used to meet on summer mornings . . . Properly to appreciate roses, [he continued], you want to see them as a setting for a girl like Angela. With her fair hair gleaming against the green leaves, she makes a rose garden seem a veritable paradise.'

In *If I Were You* Lady Lydia Bassinger and her husband Sir Herbert discuss their nephew Anthony, 5th Earl of Droitwich, and Violet Wadsworth with the Hon. Freddie Chalk-Marshall. Sir Herbert suspects that they are engaged, since he has seen them kissing in the rose garden.

> Lady Lydia uttered a feverish exclamation. 'In the rose-garden? Ye Gods! And you call that evidence! Didn't your mother teach you *anything* about the facts of life? Don't you know that everybody kisses everybody in rose-gardens?'
>
> 'How do you know?' asked Sir Herbert jealously.
>
> 'Never mind!'
>
> Freddie raised a soothing hand.
>
> 'Don't worry,' he said. 'This was one of those special kisses . . . *Lingering* . . .'
>
> 'Ah?' said Lady Lydia, dreamily. 'One of those?'
>
> 'Besides I could tell from the look on Tony's face.'
>
> 'Rapturous?'
>
> 'Half rapturous and half apprehensive. Like you see on a feller's face when he is signing a long lease for premises that he knows he hasn't inspected very carefully.'
>
> Sir Herbert puffed meditatively.

'Well, I hope you're right, by Jove! Think of Tony married to the heiress of Waddington's Ninety-Seven Soups! Whew! It's like striking an oil-gusher!'

Lady Lydia was still doubtful. 'I don't want to damp your pretty enthusiasm, Herbert,' she said, 'but I confess I should feel easier in my mind if he had kissed her somewhere else except the rose-garden. I know those rose-gardens.'

Lady Lydia was quite correct in assuming that a kiss in a rose garden was essentially unserious, since Tony married manicurist Polly Brown.

Counselling the post-First World War flapper generation on how to avoid an unwelcome declaration of love in *No Nice Girl Swears*, an etiquette book published in 1933, Alice-Leone Moats considers the garden a danger zone. Her advice is to see to it that the potential lover 'never has the opportunity to explain his feelings' and 'Avoid romantic atmosphere: moonlit gardens, deserted beaches and evenings alone in front of the fire.'

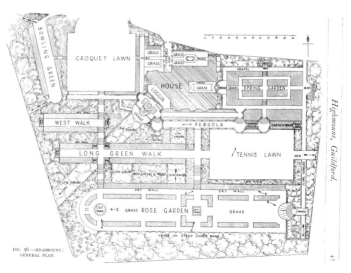

Plan for Highmount, near Guildford, from *Gardens for Small Country Houses* by Gertrude Jekyll and Lawrence Weaver, 1913. The Rose Garden lies at the far edge of the garden beyond the tennis lawn.

7   A PLACE FOR CHILDREN

Gardens are places of escape for children: spaces in which to run free, duck out of the watchful adult gaze and let their imaginations run wild. Central to their enjoyment of such a place is often the creation of a camp or base, where children can be in control of their worlds and make up their own rules. But there has always been an imbalance between what parents think children want and what they actually do.

GARDENING FOR CHILDREN

Gardening is the most unchildlike of occupations, offering little quick gratification apart from that of buying optimistically coloured packets of seeds. 'Mary, Mary, quite contrary, how does your garden grow?' Silver bells and cockle shells seem an excellent idea to children faced with a newly seeded patch of bare brown earth. However, Victorian writers pressed on with the idea that children should be made into gardeners in the belief, no doubt, that it would teach them about the wonders of Nature, and therefore God; and, as growing vegetables was judged an excellent way of keeping the working man out of the pub, so would gardening keep children healthy and out of trouble. *Gardening for Children* by the Reverend C.A. Johns was published in 1848 by the Society for Promoting Christian Knowledge. It is sententious stuff with notes on different species, instructions on how make cuttings and thoughts for the budding young philanthropist. 'Even if you have no garden of your own, you will find it a great privilege to be able, when visiting

Stephen Lewis fishes in an enamel bowl 'sea' from his wooden crate 'sailing ship'. A garden in Sussex, *c.*1955.

poor neighbours, to give them hints for turning their little plots of ground to the best advantage' – an occupation that the Revd Johns describes as an 'amusement'. He goes on: 'There are very few games which boys and girls care about when they are grown up to men and women; but the little gardener will, in all probability, become a great gardener if it please God to spare his life; and the young gardener, when he is grown old, will prefer a seat under the tree that he planted when he was a boy to the richest couch that you could offer him.'

Jane Loudon continues in the same vein in *My Own Garden or The Young Gardener's Year Book*, published in 1855. The Young Gardener needed a trowel, spade, hoe, rake, three-pronged fork, watering-pot, syringe, hand and bell glasses, basket or wheelbarrow, sponge for cleaning leaves and a hammer. The list of tasks appears long and tedious. Not until chapter four are the flower beds prepared for sowing by digging, raking and manuring. She squares respect for God's creatures with successful pest eradication by insisting that crushing the magpie moth chrysalis should be done 'when they are in a torpid state as they do not then suffer pain'; with snails she states only that it is 'probable that they do not suffer pain'. When Enid Blyton wrote on gardening for children a hundred years later she devoted a chapter to 'Enemies in the Garden', and rightly spotted that tracking down the enemy might be the most amusing aspect of gardening for the average post-war child, whose reading matter was war comics and hobby making model spitfires. 'Hunt for snails, if you suspect them of robbing your plants'; on millipedes: 'You may catch these enemies by burying a potato or carrot in the ground'; earwig eradication involved a stick and an upside-down flowerpot, which, driven into the ground beside the infested plant, would create a dark hiding place for them – 'You will catch dozens that way'. Boiling water and a good fire are her chosen methods of death, with no safety warnings. I can vouch for the pleasures of murder, having spent happy mornings as a child in the 1950s employed to catch cabbage white butterflies at a halfpenny each.

Ten-year-old orphan Mary Lennox in Frances Hodgson Burnett's *The Secret Garden* (1911) shows an enthusiastic commitment to gardening that might have warmed the hearts of the Reverend Johns and Jane Loudon, but the implausible description of her satisfaction in weeding round the snowdrops on a cold windy day is surely the voice of the middle-aged author, a passionate gardener who often wrote in her garden.

Mistress Mary worked in her garden until it was time to go to her midday dinner. In fact she was rather late in remembering, and when she put on her coat and hat and picked up her skipping-rope, she could not believe that she had been working two or three hours. She had been actually happy all the time; and dozens and dozens of tiny, pale green points were to be seen in cleared places, looking twice as cheerful as they had looked before when the grass and weeds had been smothering them.

ENGAGING WITH NATURE

When, though, Mary introduces the invalid Colin Craven to the secret garden and his rehabilitation begins, there is a passage that is recognizably a real childhood experience:

He would lie on the grass 'watching things growing', he said. If you watched long enough, he declared, you could see buds unsheathe themselves. Also you could make the acquaintance of strange, busy insect things running about on various unknown but evidently serious errands, sometimes carrying tiny scraps of straw or feather or food, or climbing blades of grass as if they were trees from whose tops one could look out to explore the country. A mole throwing up its mound at the end of its burrow and making its way out at last with the long-nailed paws, which looked so like elfish hands, had absorbed him one whole morning.

'The beech tree by night', remembered by Gwen Raverat. 'Altogether the Sandwalk was a dangerous place if you were alone.'

A child's ability to focus on minutiae is evident in Gwen Raverat's memoir *Period Piece* when she describes the garden of her grandparents, Charles and Emma Darwin, at Down in Kent:

Everything there was different. And better. For instance, the path in front of the veranda was made of large round water-worn pebbles from some sea beach. They were black and shiny, as if they had been polished. I adored these pebbles. I mean literally *adored*; worshipped. This passion made me feel quite sick sometimes . . . Long after I have forgotten all my human loves I shall still remember the smell of a gooseberry leaf, or the feel of the wet grass on my bare feet; or the pebbles in the path.

She also remembers how Charles Darwin's Sandwalk could be transformed into somewhere terrifying:

There were two or three great old trees beside the path, too, which were all right if some grown-up person were there, but much too impressive if one were alone. The Hollow Ash was mysterious enough; but the enormous beech, which we called the Elephant Tree, was quite awful. It had something like the head of a monstrous beast growing out of the trunk where a branch had been cut off. I tried to think it merely grotesque and rather funny, in the daytime; but if I were alone near it, or sometimes in bed at night, the face grew and grew until it became the mask of a kind of brutish ogre, huge, evil and prehistoric; a face which chased me down long passages and never quite caught me . . .

Exploring the garden alone is also a child's first independent move. In *Cider with Rosie,* Laurie Lee recalls the sense of being a very small child exploring his garden universe:

Through the long summer ages of those first few days I enlarged my world and mapped it in my mind, its secure havens, its dust-deserts and puddles, its peaks of dirt and flag-flying bushes. Returning too, dry-throated, over and over again, to its several well-prodded horrors: the bird's gaping bones in its cage of old sticks; the black flies in the corner, slimy dead; dry rags of snakes; and the crowded, rotting, silent-roaring city of a cat's grub-captured carcass.

The maid Martha in *The Secret Garden* remonstrates with Mary when she says that she has nothing to play with and tells of her own brothers and sisters: 'Nothing to play with! Our children plays with sticks and stones. They just runs about an' shouts at things.' Being noisy and out of control has always been a major garden attraction for children. Francis Kilvert, in the role of a young uncle, describes in his diary a Saturday afternoon in Mitcham in January 1870: 'After the boys had done lessons at 11.30, we had a good game of football, Owen, Hugh and I against Perch and Llewellyn. After luncheon we made a fortress in the faggot pile, one party defending, the others attacking, fir cones, stumps, and pieces of wood flying thick . . . A pig was descried on the lawn and hunted off precipitately.' However, childish anarchy tends to be bad for neighbourly relations. An entry from *The Diary of a Nobody* by George and Weedon Grossmith, published in 1892, tells of a Sunday morning, when the narrator, Charles Pooter, has a hangover:

> Owing, I presume, to the unsettled weather, I awoke with the feeling that my skin was drawn over my face as tight as a drum. Walking round the garden with Mr. and Mrs. Treane, members of our congregation who had walked back with us, I was much annoyed to find a large newspaper full of bones on the gravel-path, evidently thrown over by those Griffin boys next door; who, whenever we have friends, climb up the empty steps inside their conservatory, tap at the windows, making faces, whistling, and imitating birds.

Weedon Grossmith's illustration of the Griffin boys leering from next door at the Pooters and their guests.

The ability of children to create playthings out of nothing was noted by Joseph Strutt, writing on the history of English sports and pastimes at the turn of the nineteenth century, and therefore describing what pre-Industrial

Revolution children did to amuse themselves. One section in his book involves playing with inoffensive insects:

> The chafers, or May-flies, a kind of beetle found upon the bloom of hemlock in the months of May and June, are generally made the victims of youthful cruelty . . . crammed into small boxes without food, and carried in the pockets of schoolboys to be taken out and tormented at their leisure, which is done in this manner; a crooked pin having two or three yards of thread attached to it, is thrust through the tails of the chafer and on its being thrown into the air it naturally endeavours to fly away, but is readily drawn back by the boy, which occasions it to redouble its efforts to escape; these struggles are called spinning, and the more it makes of them, and the quicker the vibrations are, the more its young tormentor is delighted with his prize.

These children were not the first or the last to amuse themselves by tormenting harmless insects, and in a pre-conservation world dropping butterflies into killing jars was encouraged as an improving hobby.

IMAGINARY GAMES

The river that ran through Gwen Raverat's Cambridge garden provided water and islands for her two brothers and sister to play imaginary pirates games and Wicked French Governesses: 'Sometimes we made bonfires, and rushed about the islands waving torches made of the straw covers of wine bottles; or we had battles with miniature fire-boats, made out of cardboard boxes and candle-ends and matches.'

There was probably much less fun to be had in a sooty town garden, where playing out was more interestingly done in the street. Children's novels often illustrate how children's imagination can be prompted by space to roam. In Mrs Molesworth's *Palace in the Garden*, published in 1887, her three protagonists are sent by their guardian grandfather, who is busy and wants to go and live in his club, to a house called Rosebuds, which has a garden to play in. Here the children escape the tyranny of walks with their rheumatic nurse and are free to do as they choose and explore the garden. The 'place of places' was the tangle or the shrubbery, where they find a summer house, 'though a rather unhappy looking one' made with fir branches and cones. "'It would be a nice place for a robber's castle," said Gerald, who had mounted up beside Tib, and was peeping out at a little slit in the side wall. "See here, this hole would just do for an archer to shoot through . . ."' His sister Tib, influenced by a book called *The Imprisoned Heiress*, sees it as a place where a beautiful lady might be shut up by a cruel baron who wanted to get all her money by forcing her to marry his hump-backed son. The children find the almost obligatory door in the wall, very old and strong and covered in ivy . . .

E. Nesbit's trio of children in *The Wonderful Garden* of 1911 have parents in India and live with marginally less disagreeable guardians, vegetarians whose house is 'not papered, but distempered in clean pale tints, and the general effect was rather like that of a very superior private hospital', an impression enhanced by the fact that the floors are washed every week with Sanitas. They are sent to spend their holidays in the country at Uncle Charles's Manor House. Once arrived, they lose no time in finding the secret passage to their enclosed garden with an ancient gate carved with the date 1589 and the motto 'Here Be Dreames. Respice Finem'. Their games are rather less prosaic than those of Mrs Molesworth's children, involving such adventures as making wax effigies of a mysterious man from candle ends and creating a pagan brick altar. As their homemade incense, 'the starry gold of St. John's Wort, the gay brightness

'Nothing much happened except smoke': illustration by H.R. Miller of the three children burning offerings on their altar in *The Wonderful Garden*.

of Indian pinks, and the feathery greenness of the tamarisks twisted and writhed amid flames and smoke' they incant 'Please, Murdstone man, let your crimes and your animosity and your aversion be burnt away.' Their base is a wigwam made from three hop poles, three red blankets and their three mackintoshes.

CHILDREN'S HOUSES

There is a vast divide between the 'houses' that are presented to children by adults – usually a miniature imitation of the grown-up world – and ephemeral creations children make themselves. The most famous and oldest tree house in Britain is recorded in 1692, a half-timbered confection built into an ancient lime tree at Pitchford Hall in Shropshire, originally almost certainly intended for adults. Rebuilt in the eighteenth century, it was visited by Queen Victoria on 28 October 1832. Aged thirteen, an only child accompanied by her mother, she recorded in her journal the following impression: 'At a little past one we came home and walked about the grounds and I went up a staircase to a little house in a tree.' From its height she did nothing more exciting than watch the local hunt run by and apparently the tree house held no magic for the young princess.

The same year the Duke of Bedford built Endsleigh, his cottage ornée in Devon, and commissioned a special cottage for his children; according to Humphry Repton, who worked there, 'at this enchanting retreat the most pleasing attention has been paid to the Comforts of Infancy and Youth, of which the Children's Cottage is one of the most perfect examples'. The plate in *Sketches and Hints* accompanying Repton's words shows two boys bowling hoops on the lawn – an occupation which Strutt describes as 'much in practice at present, and especially in London, where the boys appear with their hoops in the public streets, and sometimes very troublesome to those who are passing through them'. During the same period Lord Newborough's seven children at Glynllifon in north Wales had a small turreted boathouse, complete with lavatory, a pool for their pet otter and a children's mill, inside which were small stone tables and chairs.

The educational aspects of infancy and youth seemed characteristically uppermost in Prince Albert's mind when considering the amusement of his children. He and Queen Victoria built a seaside house at Osborne on the Isle of Wight, in the grounds of which he provided his children with their own miniature universe. The intentions seem alarmingly worthy and were entirely in keeping with current beliefs on what was good for children, although maybe for the nine royal princes and princesses what the project achieved did amount to some kind of freedom. It began in 1853 with a wooden chalet imported from Switzerland which was reassembled by estate carpenters.

Official photograph taken in June 1933 of Princess Elizabeth aged seven, at the door of her Welsh cottage.

Around it was the children's own garden, complete with thatched tool shed in which were kept their miniature tools, marked with their individual initials. A housekeeper was installed, and the girls were taught how to do basic domestic tasks and cook on a dwarf range, buying their groceries from a miniature shop, Spratt's. The boys learnt carpentry and gardening and sold their produce to Prince Albert at market prices for use in the royal household. Military additions were built: Victoria Fort, a mock fortress with cannons and a drawbridge, and Albert Barracks, all of which the princes helped to construct (but surely not name). A second Swiss chalet was then erected in order to house the children's collection of natural history objects. A garden museum was very much in the spirit of the times and J.C. Loudon pointed out that what he termed an easily erected 'rustic edifice' was extremely useful in suburban gardens for displaying 'statues, minerals, models or other object', and also for children's parties, which were much better confined to the garden.

The royal children continued to enjoy enviably luxurious play houses. The people of Wales presented Princess Elizabeth with a miniature house, complete with Welsh dresser and running water, which was erected at

For the Princess's contemporaries: 'If you have young children, and wish to encourage them to stay in the open air, build them a cubby-hole' was the advice of Sid G. Hedges in *The Universal Book of Hobbies and Handicrafts*.

Windsor and which, in turn, was played in by her children. Prince Charles continued the tradition with a tree house at Highgrove for Princes William and Harry, built in 1988 up in an old holly tree with a holly-leaf-shaped door.

'A somewhat costly toy' was how the childless but imaginative Gertrude Jekyll describes a play house in *Children and Gardens*, which she wrote at the age of sixty-five in 1908. As befitted a colleague of the architect Sir Edwin Lutyens, she wrote that it should be 'a real well-built little house, with kitchen and a parlour, where they can keep house and cook and receive their friends'. Refreshingly, however, she points out that it was not only the thousands of little girls in England but small boys too who would delight in scone baking, cooking eggs and making a fire in the miniature fireplace – though the boys may not have showed so much enthusiasm for the laundering of dolls' clothes, which she also describes enthusiastically: 'In the play-house pantry, or better still, in summer weather somewhere near but out-of-doors, we wash the dollies' clothes. If the sun is very hot we put on our sun-bonnets, and we pin ourselves up in bath-towels so that no splash matters, and turn up our sleeves as high as they will go . . .'

For a poor Victorian country child such play houses were obviously a world away, but Flora Thompson wrote vividly about her 'house' in the family's cottage garden. The door of the living room was permanently open to the garden, where

one corner was given up to a tangle of currant and gooseberry bushes and raspberry canes surrounding an old apple tree. This jungle, as their father called it, was only a few feet square, but a child of five or seven could hide there and pretend it was lost, or hollow out a cave in the greenery and call it its house. Their father kept saying that he must get busy and lop the old unproductive apple tree and cut down the bushes to let in the light and air, but he was so seldom at home in daylight that for a long time nothing was done about it and they still had their hidy-houses and could still swing themselves up and ride astride on the low-hanging limb of the apple tree. From there they could see the house and their mother going in and out, banging mats and rattling pails and whitening the flagstones around the doorway.

Flora Thompson's idea of a 'hidy-house' could not be more different from that imagined by H.H. Monro, who wrote short stories under the name of Saki. He was born in the same decade as Flora Thompson, but unlike her had a miserable childhood being brought up in his grandmother's house in a villa near Barnstaple by two warring and emotionally confused aunts. His short story 'Sredni Vashtar', published in *The Chronicles of Clovis* in 1911, is based on this household. Conradin is ten, unloved and unwanted. His salvation lies in the dull and cheerless garden, where

> In a forgotten corner . . . almost hidden behind a dismal shrubbery, was a disused tool-shed of respectable proportions, and within its walls Conradin found a haven, something that took on the varying aspects of a playroom and a cathedral. He had peopled it with a legion of familiar phantoms, evoked partly from fragments of history and partly from his own brain, but it also boasted two inmates of flesh and blood. In one corner lived a ragged-plumaged Houdan hen, on which the boy lavished an affection that had scarcely another outlet. Further back in the gloom stood a large hutch . . . this was the abode of a large polecat-ferret, which a friendly butcher-boy had once smuggled, cage and all, into its present quarters, in exchange for a long-secreted hoard of small silver. Conradin was most dreadfully afraid of the lithe sharp-fanged beast, but it was his most treasured possession . . . Every Thursday in the dim and musty silence of

the tool-shed he worshipped with mystic and elaborate ceremonial before the wooden hutch where dwelt Sredni Vashtar, the great ferret.

The Wendy house was an early example of popular toys emerging from children's literature or entertainment. In the play *Peter Pan* by J.M. Barrie, which Barrie later turned into a book, a house is made for Wendy to recuperate in after the Lost Boy Tootles nearly kills her by shooting her with an arrow. Wendy sings: 'I wish I had a darling house, / The litt'lest ever seen, /With funny little red walls, /And roof of mossy green ... Gay windows all about, /With roses peeping in you know, /And babies peeping out.' The play was a huge success, and after its first production in 1904 innumerable would-be Wendy Darlings of Kensington clamoured for their own Wendy house in the garden, which the market duly provided. As the original house on stage had to be constructed during the thirty-six bars of Wendy's song, a tent-like construction was devised with rods and fabric – John's top hat provides the chimney and the sole of a shoe a door knocker – which was easily reproduced by entrepreneurial toy manufacturers. Barrie claimed that the wash house behind his childhood home in Kirriemuir was the original inspiration for Wendy's house, a far cry presumably from the toys that appeared in countless gardens of the Home Counties and beyond.

Mabel Lucie Atwell's illustration of Peter Pan in front of Wendy's house, having fallen asleep, sword drawn, while guarding her.

PRACTICAL GARDENS

As well as a place for the imagination to run riot, Gertrude Jekyll saw that the garden was a place for children to defy convention. Whereas Gwen Raverat wrote of the anguish that she felt at seeing photographs of her and her brothers and sister playing in the garden in the 1890s in high summer wearing thick, black, woolly stockings and high boots, and always with a hat to ward off cold or sunstroke, Jekyll was able to write in 1908 in *Children and Gardens*: 'There can be no doubt that the proper place for our shoes and stockings is on or near a garden bench, where we kicked or grabbed them off . . . How happy we are nowadays that we can be allowed the comfort of going barefoot.'

A nursemaid pushes a child a swing, her freedom hampered by a white lawn pinafore, floppy bonnet and thick lisle stockings.

The year 1907 saw the foundation of the Boy Scout movement, which had the camp fire as one of its most potent and enjoyable features, and Gertrude Jekyll catches much of the practical atmosphere of scouting, presenting the garden as an equal preserve of boys and girls engaged in robust occupations of an elemental nature – fire and water being the best playthings. She describes 'all the boy sort of things' she did in her childhood, such as 'take wasps' nests after dark, and do dreadful deeds with gunpowder'. The sandpit was 'a place of everlasting joy when one is small, and even when one is growing fairly biggish'. Being fairly biggish includes the pleasure of building a castle: 'Then we put some dry grass and leaves and sticks inside, with paper under, and light it at the door hole, and have quite a fine castle on fire.' Jekyll really appreciates a good bonfire:

> . . . it makes such a nice excitement, and then there is such a good
> smell, and one has to be up to all sorts of dodges to keep out of the

smoke . . . then when it is all burnt, and the great heap of ashes is left, still with a smouldering heart of a red fire left inside, we beg some big potatoes and put them in – not too far in or they would be burnt, but far enough for them to be nicely roasted in about three-quarters of an hour.

In the same chapter, which is called 'Various Amusements' but which is really about fires, she is eloquent about the proper way to make a picnic fire, using a neat arrangement of fire bricks and burying all the paper and chicken bones in a way that would have warmed the heart of Baden-Powell, who wasn't to start the Girl Guides for another two years. On water, she enthuses about the fun to be had in a stone-built paddling pool ten feet square and two feet deep – 'Nothing is more delightful than any sort of playing with water.' Although she writes at length about gardening, she also sees the space as somewhere where children can indulge their imaginations and escape from parental or nursery care to live slightly dangerously.

As it was comforting for Flora Thompson to see her mother working around the back door, so it has been important for mothers to keep an eye on their children playing in the back garden, and the standard twentieth-century British house, with the kitchen looking out on to the back garden, made this possible. As the century went by, the space increasingly resembled a municipal recreational field with swings, slides, climbing frames and paddling pools – compensation for the fact, perhaps, that parental permission to play out in the street or the fields was increasingly denied.

Wheels have always played a large part in garden games: detail from a painting of a family group, by Arthur Devis, 1749.

TOYS IN THE GARDEN

Early family portraits with a garden backdrop show children playing with hobby horses and small carts, easily identifiable as the predecessors of model cars and bikes. Vulcanized rubber was invented for motor tyres but incidentally revolutionized balls in the late nineteenth century; during the twentieth, progressive inventions of synthetic rubber and plastics led to such an explosion of toys on the market that it became a simple matter to reduce the garden to a graveyard of discarded amusements.

The range of what Victorian children might have played with in the garden is copiously listed and codified in books such as *The Boy's Own Book: A Complete Encyclopedia of all the Diversions, athletic, scientific, and recreative, of Boyhood and Youth* (1855). 'Minor Sports' comprise games with marbles, tops and balls; sports of agility, strength and speed; and sports with toys, which include a range of weaponry plucked from history and geography lessons –

Aunt Betsy's straw hat is wrecked by the ingenious Master Alfred and friends using it for target practice. A *Punch* cartoon by John Leech, 1855.

the cross-bow, pop-gun, watch-spring gun, pea-shooter, sling, boomerang, skip-jack (catapult). Still-familiar games such as hopscotch, hide and seek, quoits, bowls, swinging and see-saw are explained as well as now-forgotten ones such as tip-cat, jingling, pall mall, the living orrery and baste the bear. Mrs Gaskell describes the detritus of toys and games left lying on the lawn by Victorian children in a scene in *North and South*. When Margaret Hale returns to the vicarage where she grew up:

> The garden, the grass-plat, formerly so daintily trim that even a stray rose-leaf seemed like a fleck on its exquisite arrangement and propriety, was strewn with children's things; a bag of marbles here, a hoop there; a straw hat forced down upon a rose-tree as a peg, to the destruction of a long, beautiful, tender branch laden with flowers, which in former days would have been trained up tenderly, as if beloved.

In the child-centric world of the second half of the twentieth century more consideration was given to laying out gardens for children's amusement. The American Thomas Church suggested in *Gardens are For People* in the 1950s that the provision of 'play space with plenty of equipment, starting with a sand pile and continuing through swings, rings and slides to a basketball standard will generally keep a family of children well contented', as would a black-top path system for bicycles to enable children to ride round and round a hazard course of benches and trees, with plenty of leeway on the curves. British children of the 1960s were still offered make-do solutions by their parents such as logs for climbing frames, tractor tyres or sunk manhole drain sections filled with sand for a sandpits, but as with so much of the period, toy crazes were frequently born in America.

It was an incidental remark about Australian children whirling wooden hoops round their waists in gym classes that apparently inspired two Californians, Richard Knerr and A.K. 'Spud' Mellin, to start manufacturing in 1958 patent Marlex plastic versions, which they alluringly named Hula-Hoops. These were a spectacular craze during the British summer of 1959 and in even the smallest back garden children – and adults – could be found frantically wriggling their hips in the desired manner of Hawaiian hula dancers or Elvis Presley. Knerr and Mellin's company Wham-O simultaneously exported and developed Frisbees, which started life as empty tinfoil plates produced by the Frisbie Pie Company of Connecticut. The aerodynamic quality of the plates was serendipitously discovered by students who threw them around after finishing the pies, and plastic copies were patented as the Pluto Platter in 1948. Arriving in the midst of the moon landings, the much-loved orange and blue vinyl Space Hoppers ('amazing inflatable riding balls') further augmented the plastic quota in the back garden after 1971.

8   A PLACE TO PLAY BALL

While using the garden as a place for throwing and kicking things people have used their ingenuity to come up with a wild variety of objects to be batted, hit or thwacked from one person to another under the guise of playing games – often with surprising intensity. Grass has generally been the key to garden games, which developed in complexity and skill as rough pasture became smooth lawn. Activities once considered childish morphed into serious pastimes for grown-ups, and from the mid-nineteenth century onwards manufacturers were constantly searching for the ball that would lay a golden egg, as croquet did for Jaques & Son when the company won a gold medal at the 1851 Great Exhibition.

Figures playing bowls, from a bird's-eye view of the house and grounds of Offley House in Chauncy's *Historical Antiquities of Hertfordshire*, 1700.

Games can conflict with the gardener's desire for perfection, for precious plants are easily flattened by missiles landing and feet trampling. As games developed, so gardens were altered to accommodate them, with smooth alleys for bowling, ninepins and skittles, and wide rectangular lawns for tennis, badminton, croquet and anything else that anyone could devise. A commentator in 1890 describes how the croquet lawn came to dominate the layout of late nineteenth-century gardens; soft mossy lawns had to be beaten into submission and replaced by a 'firmer and more lively surface', for

> In default of a stronger attraction, a croquet-lawn had become the indispensable adjunct to every country house, parsonage, and villa

. . . Trees which had been the delight of the paterfamilias, and flower-beds which were to the mistresses of houses as the apple of an eye, had been ruthlessly removed to give scope for those passionate strokes which satisfied for the moment the vindictiveness of the most relentless croquet player.

BOWLS, NINEPINS AND SKITTLES

On the grandest scale, Henry VII's gardens at his palace at Richmond included in 1501 'pleasant galleries and houses of pleasure to disport in, at chess, tables, dice, cards, billiards, bowling alleys, butts for archers, and goodly tennis plays – as well to use the said plays and disports as to behold them so disporting'. His son, Henry VIII, installed 'divers fair tennice-courtes, bowling alleys, and a cock-pit' at Whitehall Palace. Real tennis courts, such as the one at Hampton Court Palace, were covered buildings. Bowling became so popular that in 1541 public bowling alleys were banned as dangerously time-wasting for the lower classes. Labourers, artisans, apprentices and servants were allowed to play bowls only during the twelve days of Christmas and then only within the confines of their masters' gardens and orchards.

The government made a useful income from the passion for bowls, since a licence to bowl in the garden had to be obtained if the land itself was worth over £100 per annum. Betting on the outcome of games was common practice. The privy purse expenses of Henry VIII record his gaming: on 29 January 1530, Mr Fitzwilliam, the treasurer, won £4 10s. off the king at bowls; on 19 April 1532, Lord Wiltshire and Lord Rocheford had to be paid £9 by the king, who also lost a steep £35 5s. to a Mr Baynton a few days later. Since it was also recorded that Lady Anne lost over £12 to the Sergeant of the Cellar, bowls was evidently not exclusively a male preserve. Such betting was still rife a century later, when Charles Cotton's *Compleat Gamester*, first issued in 1674, stated: 'A Bowling-green or Bowling-Ally is a place where three things are thrown away besides the Bowls, viz. Time, Money, and Curses, and the last ten for one.'

Gardens throughout Britain were adapted to include the required length of greensward. Some idea of the fierce passions engendered by bowling is apparent from two seventeenth-century poems on the subject. 'A Parallel betwixt Bowling and Preferment' by William Stroad exposes methods of finagling employed to win (both game and job):

> Some, whose heate and zeal exceed,
> Thrive well by rubbs that curb their haste,
> And some that languish in their speed
> Are cherished by some favour's blaste;
> Some rest in other's cutting out
> The fame by whom themselves are made;
> Some fetch a compass farr about,
> And secretly the marke invade.

Joseph Addison wrote 'Sphaeristerium' in Latin. It was translated by his contemporary, the satirical poet and pamphleteer Nicholas Amhurst, and published as 'The Bowling Green'. The poem describes the polished globes 'glittering with oil' and marked by their owners – 'For gamesters vary; some prefer the bowl/That, biassed, wheels obliquely to the goal' – and the player making the time-honoured excuse of a bad throw:

> He blames the rising-rub, and guilty ground.
> What sudden laughter echoes o'er the green,
> When some unlucky, artless cast is seen!
> When the too ponderous lead with stubborn force
> Allures the globe from its appointed course!
> The bowler chafes, and fruitless rage ensues,
> His body to a thousand postures screws:
> He blames he knows not what, with angry blood,
> He frets, he stamps, and damns the erroneous wood.

Bowling was evidently still vastly popular in the eighteenth century – so much so that in an essay on clergymen William Cowper attacked lazy clerics with a penchant for garden improvements and games for the bad condition of church buildings:

. . . the ruinous condition of some of these edifices gives me great offence; and I could not help wishing that the honest vicar, instead of indulging his genius for improvements, by enclosing his gooseberry-bushes with chinese rail, and converting half an acre of his glebe land into a bowling green, would have applied part of his income to the more laudable purpose of sheltering his parishioners from the weather during their attendance on divine service.

Ninepins and skittles required a similar garden space. At Claremont in Surrey, one of the grandest eighteenth-century gardens in England, the Duke of Newcastle had built both a bowling green and a ninepin alley (the existence of which is recorded in 1719), both arranged with garden seats alongside and, in the case of the ninepin alley, with a little temple for spectators. The duke was concerned for the condition of the grass of 'the Rolling Place' and wrote to his wife instructing her to have the overhanging

The ninepin alley at Claremont: vignette engraved by J. Rocque,
in a mid-eighteenth-century edition of *Vitruvius Britannicus*.

yew trees trimmed, since a certain standard of surface was required. On his travels through Yorkshire Richard Pococke was impressed to see at the extravagantly well-appointed Wentworth House that the Marquis of Rockingham had 'a skittle ground for the youth to divert themselves, not to omit a beautiful temple to Cloacina with a portico round it, supported by columns made of the natural trunks of trees'. Pococke was noting in his travel journal the convenience of a nearby lavatory – Cloacina being the Roman goddess of sewers. Skittle grounds could be fitted into town gardens. The antiquarian Francis Douce was advised in the 1790s by his keen gardening friend Richard Twiss that if there was insufficient sun for flowers in his Bloomsbury garden, he should settle for just a grass plat (lawn) or a skittle ground.

Games rose and fell not just in popularity but also in social status. The Duke of Newcastle's ninepin alley at Claremont was turned into flower beds by the property's subsequent owners, Princess Charlotte and Prince Leopold, because they regarded skittles as a distinctly low-grade entertainment. As Robert Huish wrote in a memoir of the princess a year after her death in childbirth in 1818, 'such low amusements . . . not being congenial to the taste of Prince Leopold, and as skittle grounds were considered rather out of character on a demesne where taste and elegance only were to be exhibited, they were, at her express desire, removed.' It seems that after this 'low' skittles were demoted to being the amusements of servants or something to be enjoyed at the pub with beer. Indeed, the Duchess of Sutherland's footman recorded in his diary in 1838: 'After hall dinner me and some more went and had a game of skittles and was playing nearly all afternoon.' He didn't relate if he had bets on this game, but he certainly did on a game of quoits that he described a few weeks later, enjoyed after a morning cleaning plate in the pantry: 'I then took a walk through the park and as I was coming back by the yard gate there was Charles, Richard the Groom and George Hawkins going to have a game of quoits. Richard and me took the other two at 3d a corner. We beat them 31 to 21. I then came in and dressed myself and laid the cloth for dinner and got to bed about 11.'

GAMES FOR THE LAWN

In the early nineteenth century the grass on bowling greens and ninepin alleys would have been trimmed by laborious scything, believed to be best done early in the morning while the dew was still on the grass. With the invention of the mechanical lawn mower this rapidly became a thing of the past and a smooth lawn was an attainable goal even for those who did not employ a large staff of gardeners. Manufacturer Thomas Green of Leeds exhibited at the 1862 International Exhibition in South Kensington and boasted: 'These machines now stand unrivalled . . . lawns can be bought to a state of perfection', and they came in several sizes suitable for small plots or extensive lawns. A New Patent Garden Roller further enhanced the surface. This development meant a radical change in what games could be played in the garden.

A sense emerges that during the 1870s the entire echelons of middle- and upper-class British society, men, women and children, were out in the garden playing games on the lawn. *Cassell's Book of Sports and Pastimes* catalogues the following as lawn games: badminton, bowls, croquet, lawn billiards, lawn tennis and quoits (as distinct from minor outdoor games, field games, hoop games, playground games and manly games). Bowls had gone out of fashion: in 1870 Francis Kilvert wrote in his diary of a lunch party, 'Afterwards we had croquet and archery and I played

Ladies playing a decorous game of badminton:
Christmas card, *c*.1890.

155

bowls with Baskerville, an old set that were rummaged out of an outhouse for the occasion, not having been used for years.'

Battledore and shuttlecock, having sometimes been played indoors, became essentially a garden game. The antiquarian Joseph Strutt called it a boyish sport of long standing and in *Sports and Pastimes of the People of England* included a reproduction showing two boys playing alongside an anecdote about James I's son, Prince Henry: 'His highness playing a shittle-cocke, with one farr taller than himself, and hittying him by chance with the shittle-cocke upon his forehead, "This is," quoth he, "the encounter of David with Goliath".' Jane Austen struggled to play the game with her nephew William, and described her attempts in a letter she wrote in Godmersham in August 1805: 'Yesterday was a very quiet day with us; my noisiest efforts were writing to Frank and playing at Battledore and Shuttlecock with William; he and I have practiced together two mornings, and improve a little; we have frequently kept it up *three* times, & once or twice *six*.'

A bustle was no hindrance to a game of battledore and shuttlecock: illustration from *The Graphic*, May 1871.

A sign of the times was the arrival of a new lawn game, which adapted the humble battledore and shuttlecock, had a higher status and rules, and, crucially, was adversarial. This was an importation from the British Raj, where 'Ladies Rackets' had been devised, to be played with a suitably soft shuttlecock rather than the usual hard ball. For uncertain reasons it was given the name badminton. Word of this game spread to Britain: enquiries in the letters page of *The Field* in the early summer of 1873 requesting information on how to play were quickly followed by the reprinting of a set of rules written by Major Forbes and published by the Great Eastern Hotel Company in Calcutta, as kindly supplied by an Indian correspondent. Within a few years badminton was an established game, but despite its enthusiastic adherents one destined always to be overshadowed by croquet and tennis, being seen primarily as one for the ladies.

The rules for croquet were written by John Jaques in 1864 and the game was an immediate success. Cassell's book gives it a dramatic introduction:

> Never, probably, has there been a game so universally and thoroughly popular in Great Britain as Croquet, and never was a popularity so rapidly achieved . . . Those who remember the first introduction of the game can alone recall to mind the sort of mania which it excited throughout the length and breadth of the land. It was the first successful attempt that had been made to invent an out-door game in which both sexes could join on terms of equality, and in which, as scarcely any muscular power was required, the weak stood almost as fair a chance of winning as the strong.

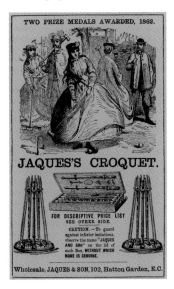

An early advertisement, dated May 1866, for a Jaques's croquet set, demonstrating clearly the intention that it should be played by men and women together.

The Duke and Duchess of Montairy, in Benjamin Disraeli's 1870 novel *Lothair*, were fashionably passionate about the game, and though he thinks himself 'the most accomplished male performer existing', the duke bows to his wife's unrivalled skill: 'she was the queen of croquet'. They give a croquet party at their country seat, Brentham, an Italianate palace with stately terraces and extensive gardens 'bright with flowers, dim with coverts of rare shrubs and musical with fountains'. The guests include:

Mr. Blenkinsop, a grave young gentleman, whose countenance never relaxed when he played, and who was understood to give his mind entirely up to croquet . . . He drove over with some fine horses and several cases and bags containing instruments and weapons for the fray. His sister came with him, who had forty thousand pounds, but, they said, was in some mysterious manner dependent on his consent to her marriage; and it was added that Mr. Blenkinsop would not allow his sister to marry because he would miss her so much in his favourite pastime.

The hero, wealthy young aristocrat Lord Lothair, assesses the game in progress:

a game of great deliberation and of more interest than gaiety, though sometimes a cordial cheer, and sometimes a ringing laugh of amiable derision, notified a signal triumph or a disastrous failure. But the scene was brilliant: a marvellous lawn, the Duchess's Turkish tent with its rich hangings, and the players themselves, the prettiest of all the spectacle, with their coquettish hats, and their half-veiled and half-revealed under-raiment, scarlet and silver, or blue and gold, made up a sparkling and modish scene.

Disraeli's scene has echoes of a medieval tournament, suiting the determinedly competitive, even antagonistic flavour of the game.

The fashionable young man in George Eliot's novel *Daniel Deronda* is similarly enthusiastic, saying: 'depend upon it croquet is the game of the future. It wants writing up though. One of our best men has written a poem on it, in four cantos: – as good as Pope. I want him to publish it. You never read anything better.'

The tremendous enthusiasm for croquet, and subsequently for tennis, is evident in the diaries of Francis Kilvert, written while he was a young churchman living on the Welsh borders. He makes frequent reference to social events during the 1870s built round the games. Tuesday, 12 July 1870: 'Great fun on the lawn, six cross games of croquet and balls flying in all directions. High tea at 7.30. More than forty people sat down. Plenty

Cartoon published in the humorous journal *Judy*, pointing up the opportunities for ankle display – and jealousy – engendered by croquet.

of iced claret cup, and unlimited fruit, very fine, especially the strawberries . . . the ladies' light dresses looked ghostly in the dusk and at a little distance it was almost impossible to tell which was a lady in a white dress and which was a clump of tall white lilies.' Four days later he plays in the dark 'a wild nonsensical game . . . everyone playing at the same time, and screams of laughter which might be heard almost in Hay.' Undoubtedly much of the game's popularity was due largely to the fact that men and women played together in pairs, thus allowing for all sorts of interesting social encounters.

TENNIS

The supremacy of croquet came to be challenged by tennis: in the rather histrionic words of the lawn tennis volume of the *Badminton Library of Sports and Pastimes* (1890), tennis 'extinguished croquet as easily as the Greek hero crushed the Erymanthian boar'. The London *Court Journal* noted the 'arrival' of lawn tennis in a piece that appeared on 7 March 1874:

> We hear of a new and interesting game coming out, which is likely to attract public notice, now blasé with croquet and on the *qui vive* for novelty. It has been patented under the name of 'Sphairistike (Greek – belonging to the game of ball) or lawn tennis'. It has been tested in several country houses, and has been found full of healthy excitement, besides being capable of much scientific play. The game is in a box not much larger than a double gun case, and contains, besides bats and balls, a portable court, which can be erected on any ordinary lawn.

An Edwardian tennis party in full swing, with young women running athletically for the ball: painting by Charles Gere.

Probably the Hercules behind this puff for the new game was Major Walter Clopton Wingfield, an entrepreneurial guards officer and efficient publicist. He aimed to cash in by modernizing the ancient game of tennis and adapting it to garden lawns already smoothed for croquet. He patented the name Sphairistike (which was quickly dropped – it had been shortened to 'Sticky' and did not trip from the tongue of those lacking a classical education). Having organized friendly editorials in *The Field* and the *Army and Navy Gazette*, he published 'Wingfield's Rules of the Game' and simultaneously arranged for boxed tennis sets, including bouncing rubber balls, to be ready for instant dispatch from Messrs French & Co. in London.

In the summer of 1874 Kilvert noted the purchase of a new lawn mower manufactured by Follows and Bates, price £4 2s. 6d, and tried out the new game: 'This morning Teddy set up the net and poles in the field just opposite the dining room windows and we began to play 'sphairistike" or lawn tennis, a capital game, but rather too hot for a summer's day.' The mid-1870s saw chaos, with competing rules and various claimants saying that they had been playing lawn tennis for ages and that it wasn't a new game at all. The Bishop of Bath and Wells said he had been playing it on his rectory lawn in Suffolk with his family and guests for years, since he had felt playing real tennis was unsuitable for a cleric. However, the Marylebone Cricket Club was called in and a definitive set of rules was established in 1875.

PERFECT WHITENESS

The white frocks of summer—tennis, school, and beach frocks—keep their immaculate purity when washed with Omo. Stains cannot resist its cleansing. Even after countless washings Omo brings back unfailingly that lasting, dazzling whiteness. And so easily done, for with Omo you simply boil. It bleaches while washing—and does both safely, *thoroughly*.

Safe Bleacher **OMO** *and Cleanser*

You need only boil

Realization of Lottie Dod's dream, 1929: maybe not bare legs but certainly a dress guaranteeing easy movement and laundering.

For women, tennis was satisfyingly more active than croquet and, according to Lottie Dod in 1890, 'provided a delightful and healthy exercise, of which ladies had long felt the want'. A Wimbledon champion who first won the tournament at the age of fifteen, she wrote in the *Badminton* volume: 'Ladies should learn to run, and run their hardest too, not merely stride.' She added: 'Ladies' dress, too, is a matter for grave consideration; for how can they ever hope to play a sound game when their dresses impede the free movement of every limb? In many cases their very breathing is rendered difficult. A suitable dress is sorely needed.' Tennis and bicycling allowed women to escape from the constricting fashions of the late nineteenth century. Badminton and croquet could be played with bustle, tight waist and fashionable hat, but tennis could not. Female competitiveness had been honed on the croquet pitch but tennis allowed women to display a hitherto unexpressed energy and verve.

Thomas Hardy includes a garden party in *A Laodicean*, written in 1881 at the height of the tennis craze, describing 'some young people who were so madly devoted to lawn-tennis that they set about it like day-labourers at the moment of their arrival'. However, the athleticism of tennis made a negative impression on the older generation, who sought peace in the garden. E.F. Benson makes his disapproval evident in a passage in the late Victorian novel *Dodo*:

> The thump of tennis balls, the flying horrors of ring-goal, even the clash of croquet is tabooed in this sacred spot. Down below, indeed, beyond that thick privet hedge, you may find, if you wish, a smooth, well-kept piece of grass, where, even now – if we may judge from white figures that cross the little square, where a swinging iron gate seems to remonstrate hastily and ill-temperedly with those who leave these reflective shades for the glare and publicity of tennis – a game seems to be in progress.

Social games of tennis and croquet could be drawn out. In *Period Piece* Gwen Raverat describes the boredom she and her siblings felt during long games of croquet, as a result of which they devised Tennicroque, whereby they threw tennis balls at croquet ones to make them move. Waiting and watching demanded new types of garden furnishings and buildings in the way of shelters, seats and benches. Young men could throw themselves on the grass, but decorum dictated that young women did not. Folding croquet or tennis seats, some with comfortable carpet seats and easily carried to the scene of the action, appear in the catalogues of the time. One manufacturer produced a garden bench with a box built into the seat for storing croquet mallets and balls. A *Country Life* editorial in a summer issue of 1905 approved:

THE BRITISH CHARACTER.
IMPORTANCE OF BEING ATHLETIC.

'Instead of thoughts, the English have traditions': one of Pont's pre-war cartoons from *Punch*, published in book form in 1938 with an introduction by E.M. Delafield.

Everyone knows what a nuisance it is, having decided to spend the next two hours over a game of croquet, to be obliged to go back to the house and bring out armfuls of mallets, balls, and clips, which insist on dropping and rolling away down the path, and which necessitate a great deal more exercise than is compatible with keeping cool. It makes all the difference to find everything ready to hand on the lawn, and the garden seat with box, should appeal to the laziness, the legitimate laziness, of everyone on a hot July day.

This was a costly £6 in oiled teak (lock 5s. extra).

Tennis parties became popular social events for summer weekend afternoons. The scene of a tennis party impresses in the *Diary of a Provincial*

Lady by E.M. Delafield, which chronicles upper-middle-class life in rural Devon in 1930:

> Tennis-party at wealthy and elaborate house, to which Robert and I now bidden for the first time. (Also probably, the last.) Immense opulence of host and hostess at once discernible in fabulous display of deck-chairs, all of complete stability and miraculous cleanliness . . . Elderly, but efficient looking, partner is assigned to me, and we play against the horn-rimmed spectacles and agile young creature in expensive crepe-de-chine. Realise at once that all three play very much better tennis than I do. Still worse, realise that *they* realise this. Just as we begin, my partner observes gravely that he ought to tell me he is a left-handed player. Cannot imagine what he expects me to do about it, lose my head, and reply madly, that That is Splendid.

Tennis lawns proliferated in country and suburban houses wherever space was available, but the frustrations of the English climate with slippery grass, wet balls on gut-strung racquets and chalky white boundary lines obliterated by a couple of hours of rain were considerable for keen players. The solution was a hard tennis court, and the *Country Life* publication *The House and its Equipment* (1911) gave instructions on how to build one for what it termed the 'supreme game of give and take'. Year-round tennis playing would allow players to improve their game and 'more men of promise be discovered to graduate eventually at Wimbledon and represent us against Colonial cousins'. Whether the contemplation of such a starry future was the impetus for many garden owners to lay six inches of gas clinker, roll it with a heavy horse roller, and then cover this with a layer of three inches of burnt clay ballast rolled down with a lighter roller pulled by three men it is difficult to judge. The author is reassuring that 'any agricultural labourer or gardener can easily do the work'. The hard tennis court company of En-Tout-Cas, founded in 1909, simplified life for those without recourse to plenty of labour.

Pages from *The Universal Book of Hobbies* put out in the 1920s and aimed at a suburban market where space was limited demonstrate that a certain amount of ingenuity was required to adapt a back lawn for games.

Announcing that 'Even if your lawn is very small there are plenty of games you can play on it, many of them quite as good as tennis,' it suggests putting up old fishing nets to protect your neighbours from flying balls and using tape to mark out a court. For small lawns ring tennis (with a sponge rubber ring), padder tennis (with solid wood racket and sponge ball), tether shuttle (with shuttlecock tethered to central net, so as not to inconvenience the neighbours) or toss ball (a version of volleyball) are all recommended. Old motor tyres ('very useful for a great many lawn games, it is worth while

Outdoor games proposed for small back gardens by Sid G. Hedges in *The Universal Book of Hobbies*: left pole tennis, right horseshoe tossing.

keeping a few on hand') could be adapted for tyre quoits and tyre target. In the latter, sticks, balls and pebbles were thrown through the tyre as it was rolled from one end of the lawn to the other. One needed only to purchase a few horseshoes from the local blacksmith to play horseshoe ringing, an adaptation of quoits.

The world of the suburban back garden, 'where the rituals of the family outdoors could be enacted, from the cutting of the grass on Saturday evenings with the Ransome's hand-pushed mower to the hanging out of clothes on wash-day Monday', was described in *Dunroamin* by Paul Oliver, who was bought up in Rayner's Lane, north of London between the wars: 'The rear garden was the realm in which children could play, the wife could sunbathe, a husband could practise his tennis strokes or the family play clock golf and French cricket.' At this period local tennis and golf clubs were growing in popularity, so the garden was simply for practising swings and strokes. The firm of Jaques had introduced clock golf, and in response to golfers' needs had added to a range of equipment, involving nets and putting holes and designed to soften the blow of not having space for eighteen holes at the back of the house. Inspired by the French, boules had also been added to the repertoire of garden games, conveniently playable on any surface.

Games on the lawn never change in spirit. In an atmospheric description which recalls Addison's 'Bowling Green' poem, Alison Adburgham, writing in *Punch* in 1955, remembers:

> . . . you do not need to be more than middle-aged to remember games that went on so long in the deepening dusk that a croquet-maddened father, bitten by the game as badly as his guests by the evening midges, would call for the stable lamps to be brought out to light the hoops . . . or other summer evenings when, guests departed, the children would be loosed on the court for a quick round of Golf Croquet, or better still a harum-scarum of Crazy Croquet before they went to bed.

Boxed set of putters, holes and balls for practising golf in the garden. Manufactured by Slazenger, early twentieth century.

9   A PLACE FOR DISPLAY, PARTIES AND PERFORMANCES

A garden is unlikely to be for the pleasure of its creator alone. Gardens are made for sharing with friends, the public or just random passers-by. People have done and can do wonderfully varied things with spaces both large and small. And these are not all to do with plants. When driving or walking past it is impossible not be entertained by eccentric and surprising gardens, full of miniature buildings, gnome families, plaster-figured cricket matches, small-scale railways or cement menageries, or adorned with enough Christmas decorations and lights to blow the national grid. Coach parties made detours to see the miniature village that Jack Miles created in his front garden in the Wiltshire village of Downton. Frequently such attention-grabbing is put to good use with a collecting box or wishing well positioned to collect money for a good cause. It is a small example of

A plate from Repton's *Sketches and Hints on Landscape Gardening* of Brandsbury in Middlesex, 1794. He urged the removal of the long fence to ensure open views.

what happens on a large scale with the National Gardens Scheme, or when a village fête is held on the vicarage lawn. And the garden party has long been a fixture of the British summer, weather permitting.

INVITING IN THE PUBLIC

The gardens of Tudor palaces, such as those at Hampton Court and Theobalds, were divided into the Great Garden, the splendour of which was for the benefit of the wider world, and the Privy Garden, reserved for the very few. Humphry Repton, as the leading landscape gardener of the late eighteenth century, was quite firm in his opinion that gardens were for everyone, writing, 'For the honour of the country, let the Parks and Pleasure Grounds of England be ever open to cheer the hearts and delight the eyes of all, who have taste to enjoy the beauties of nature.' In one of his books he illustrated the frustration of being excluded from a satisfying glimpse of a garden view with three figures peering over and through a fence. People are generally very curious, even if the beauty of nature is possibly not the prime motive for everyone.

Earlier in the century, Alexander Pope had created what was a source of fascination for many and made to be seen. He acquired a villa and five acres of land in Twickenham in 1719 and made a garden with groves, a wilderness, a bowling green, an amphitheatre, a shell temple, an obelisk, an orangery and a vineyard. By the river he had a sequence of monuments including ones to the classical poets Virgil and Homer (particularly apt since Pope had translated the *Iliad*) and reclining river gods. The most dazzling feature was a grotto, which amazed his peers. This was a virtue made from a necessity, involving the elaborate decoration of a tunnel that ran under the main road and linked the Thames riverside to his house and garden. The conversion of tunnel to grotto was a sparkling tour de force: side rooms were hewn out of the straight passageway and the walls were decorated with a mosaic comprising shards of mirror glass, shells, crystals, quartzes, minerals and stalactites, the latter infamously shot down from Wookey Hole. A stream trickled through, adding the echoing sound of running water to the experience. Pope was particularly pleased with the way in which he could change the light effects. He wrote to his friend Edward Blount on its completion in 1725:

> When you shut the doors of this grotto, it becomes on the instant, from a luminous room, a camera obscura on the walls of which all objects of the river – hills, woods and boats – are forming a moving picture . . . and when you have a mind to light it up it affords you a different scene. It is finished with shells, interspersed with pieces of looking glass in angular form, and in the ceiling is a star of the same material, at which, when a lamp is hung in the middle, a thousand pointed rays glitter, and are reflected all over the place.

During his lifetime Pope showed his garden to his wide social circle, who would have appreciated its poetic allusions, classical references and Latin inscriptions, and, presumably, its startling light effects. After his death in 1744 its fame spread to the general public, an account appearing, for example, in the *Newcastle General Magazine* for January 1748. The garden became a victim of its extraordinariness and Pope's fame: tourists arrived and carried off the contents as souvenirs, just as predicted in a poem called 'The Cave of Pope', published by Robert Dodsley and written just before Pope died:

> Then some small Gem, or Moss, or Shining Ore,
>   Departing each shall pilfer, in fond hope
> To please their Friends, on every distant Shore
>   Boasting a Relick from the Cave of Pope.

The passion for building and improving country houses and estates during the eighteenth century was matched by an enthusiasm for visiting them. Caroline and Philip Lybbe Powys made lengthy and energetic journeys in the summer months; she noted that during three weeks in July 1760 that they had travelled 514 miles. The couple had little compunction in wandering around uninvited; at 'Burleigh Hall' (Burghley), she wrote in her diary, 'We were more fortunate than we expected, for as we were walking in the garden, standing still on a nearer approach to the house . . . Lord Exeter happened to be overlooking his workmen, and reading, as I suppose, curiosity in our countenances, politely asked if the ladies chose to see it.' Extended landscape gardens were wonders to be experienced. To tour an eighteenth-century garden was often to follow a route devised by the owner for the amusement of his friends and visitors and to flatter or test their erudition. It could, however, baffle, as Lord Orrery found; he wrote in a letter: 'To tell the truth, my tenants have a notion that I am atheistically inclined, by putting up heathen statues and writing on them certain words in an unknown language they immediately suspected me for a papist, and my statues had been demolished, my woods burnt and my throat cut had not I suddenly placed a seat under a holly bush with this plain inscription Sit Down and Welcome.'

Creators of spectacular gardens wanted them to be seen and admired by the wider world. One such garden was that of Charles Hamilton, who created a Georgian landscape garden at Painshill in Surrey and devised a sequence of 'views' to be seen from a prescribed route: a hermitage in a dark wood, a temple of Bacchus in a bucolic setting, a sham ruin, a prospect tower, a grotto, a Turkish tent and a gloomy Roman mausoleum. He had an arrangement with an inn in nearby Cobham to provide chairs drawn by ponies for those who did not feel up to walking the course; and it was in one of these that Caroline Lybbe Powys saw it in May 1778: 'We went with Miss Ewer at Clapham to see Panes Hill, late Mrs Hamilton's. The grounds are seven miles round, which we went in little chaises . . . the finest as well as the most strikingly beautiful grotto, all made of Derbyshire spar.'

A garden worth display also demonstrated the latest novelties of style, to the extent that one eighteenth-century commentator regretted the passing of the days

The Brockman family were evidently keen that the notable features of their garden at Beachborough Park in Kent, as well as people enjoying them, should be included in Edward Haytley's painting of *c*.1744.

when the price of a haunch of venison with a country friend was only half-an-hours walk on a hot terrass; a descent to two square fish-ponds overgrown with frog-spawn; a peep into the hog-sty, or a visit to the pigeon house. How reasonable was this when compared with the attention now expected from you to the number of temples, pagodas, pyramids, grottos, bridges, hermitages, caves, towers etc.

Chinoiserie was in vogue among the Georgian cognoscenti. In the 1720s views of Chinese landscape and gardens were filtering through to Europe, in particular those of the Chinese Emperor K'ang Hsi's summer palace and garden near Peking with its pavilions, grottoes, menageries, lakes and ornamental trees. Early interest was sparked by the arrival in London of an Italian Jesuit priest, Matteo Ripa, in 1724 with a set of engraved views that gave substance to the vision and specific features to imitate. Ripa

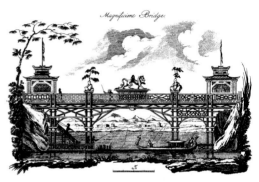

Magnificent Bridge, one of the 'elegant and useful designs' in Paul Decker's book *Chinese Architecture Civil and Ornamental*, 1759.

described the pavilions as small pleasure houses to which the emperor retired when he was tired of fishing, accompanied by his ladies. Little ephemeral chinoiserie features began to appear in gardens all over the shires. An early enthusiast was the Hon. Richard Bateman ('Dicky' to Mrs Delany), who from the 1730s created a miniature Chinese world at the Grove, Old Windsor, in Berkshire. Richard Pococke saw it on his long peripatetic summer holiday of 1754, and describes what sounds like an evocation of a willow pattern plate. Mr Bateman, it seems, had a 'charming box': a small house with four rooms on each floor and a miniature gallery measuring three feet by nine feet and filled with curious things, and a storeroom filled with Chinese and Japanese porcelain. Mrs Bateman had a separate, presumably more habitable, house in the grounds, where there was also a grove;

> and beyond that is a Chinese covered bridge to an island, and another uncovered beyond it to another island. This and the swans on the river make it a most delightful piece of scenery. Behind this house, beyond the grove, is a meadow . . . At the corner of this meadow is the farm house, with a small garden in parterre and a green house; this is in the Chinese taste; in the room below they commonly breakfast in summer.

Pococke was not, apparently, a friend of the Batemans but had been given access to the garden. Horace Walpole was a friend and it was he who later claimed to have swayed Bateman into giving the whole garden a Gothick makeover. As he put it, 'every pagoda took the veil' and the house was given an appropriate name change, becoming the Priory, which demonstrates both the fickleness of garden fashions and also the fact that after a few decades chinoiserie temples made for effect from wood and plaster were almost certainly crumbling fast.

William Shenstone's *ferme ornée*, as he termed The Leasowes, became such an attraction that Lady Luxborough wrote to him in a mildly belligerent tone in the 1750s: 'I find the Leasowes is become the resort of the *beau monde*; nor do I wonder at it; but I think the Masters of the Vauxhalls, Ranelagh and the Playhouses in the neighbourhood ought to file a bill against you, for decoying their company from them.' A full description of the Leasowes, reading in the manner of a modern guidebook, was published by Robert Dodsley in 1764, so preserving its fame.

Jonathan Tyers, owner of the public Vauxhall pleasure garden, had his own private garden called Denbies in Surrey, to which he gave a morbid Gothic theme, emphasizing the transience of life. Temples were dedicated to Death, coffins formed archways, skulls formed decorative motifs and one area was named the Valley of the Shadow of Death. More spiritually uplifting would have been the Christian garden journey created at Hough Hole House near Macclesfield by a Victorian Methodist preacher, James Mellor. Within his two acres Mellor created a circuit based on John Bunyan's *Pilgrim's Progress*, using his own imagination and ingenuity as well as practical skills. Large parties of visitors came from Manchester on Sundays, with crowds of up to five hundred on Good Friday, to follow his instructive route. On entering the front gate a visitor was invited along the Holy Way, which led quickly into the Slough of Despond (the fruit and vegetable garden, rather inappropriately). There was a Hill of Difficulty and a Bypath Meadow (which doubled as the Mellors' tennis court); Doubting Castle was the neighbouring farmhouse disguised by giant blocks of stone. Mellor created the Howling House (a by-way to hell) by building a summer house with a fireplace. Here a fire was lit, with sulphur added to give the smell of brimstone, thus illustrating the passage from Bunyan 'They looked in therefore and saw that within it was very dark and smoky; they also thought that they heard a lumbering noise as of fire, and a cry of some tormented, and they smelt the smell of brimstone.' By placing an Aeolian harp in an opening, which was activated by the draught of opening the door, Mellor also produced the cries of the disturbed souls.

PARTIES AND PERFORMANCES

A large garden can accommodate a far larger crowd than even the grandest house, a point succinctly made in a book entitled *Party-Giving on Every Scale* in 1882: 'A garden party is a popular and not expensive form of entertainment, as hospitality can be shown to a large circle of guests at a very modest cost.'

The garden party was always a useful way of entertaining royalty, as in events such as the entertainment at Elvetham for Elizabeth I, described in chapter 3; equally it has been used by royalty to entertain others. Prince Frederick held a spectacular garden event at Cliveden in Berkshire to commemorate the accession of his grandfather, George I, to the throne, as well as to celebrate the third birthday of his daughter Augusta. The date was 1 August, and the year 1740. Wishing to stress the family's Hanoverian attachment to their new country, he chose to put on a specially commissioned masque with a British theme called *Alfred*. The music was by Thomas Arne and it all ended with the enduring couplet written by James Thomson:

> Rule Britannia, rules the waves:
> Britons never will be slaves.

Alfred was staged, as the *London Daily Post and General Advertiser* described it, 'upon a theatre in the Garden compos'd of vegetables, and decorated with Festoons of Flowers, at the End of which was erected a Pavilion for their Royal Highnesses'. So entranced was the king that he commanded a repeat performance, with the addition of some of his favourite pantomime scenes, 'which was accordingly begun, but the Rain falling very heavy, oblig'd them to break off before it was half over; upon which his Royal Highness commanded them to finish the Masque of Alfred in the House'.

Such an event required extra attractions in the form of bands, plays, entertainers, outdoor ballets, and the Georgians introduced these as *fête champêtre*, the enactment of a Watteauesque French rococo fantasy. Horace Walpole claimed that that given by Lord Stanley (later Earl of Derby) in June 1774 to celebrate his engagement to Lady Elizabeth Hamilton was the first diversion of this kind in England. Lord Stanley gave it, appropriately, at Lambert's Oaks, his villa in Banstead, Surrey, which was his base for horse racing at nearby Epsom. The party began at 6.30 p.m. with rural sports and proceeded through until four in the morning with theatrical diversions, supper and a ball, and was prodigiously expensive. Rural sports were an interesting addition and evidently did not involve the guests but were there to create a visual backdrop. Around

this time David Garrick gave famous garden fêtes at his house in Hampton, where he reputedly employed local inhabitants to pose as haymakers, and old women to run races for the enjoyment of his friends. On one occasion Fox, Burke, Sheridan, Gibbon and Reynolds all looked on while an old man and youth competed to fill and empty baskets of stones.

Prince Hermann von Pückler-Muskau describes two garden parties given in the summer of 1826, equally blessed with brilliant weather and equally lavish. The sense is that the atmosphere is relaxed, even mildly louche compared to the squashes of the West End balls and drawing rooms. First he goes to a 'very pleasant rural fete' to celebrate the wedding of Harriot Coutts to the Duke of St Albans on 1 May. Harriot could afford to produce indescribably rich effects since, despite her humble beginnings as the illegitimate daughter of travelling players, her marriage to Thomas Coutts had left her an extremely wealthy widow. The prince wrote: 'At five o'clock a few blasts of a trumpet announced a splendid breakfast, at which all the delicacies and costly viands that luxury could furnish, were served in the greatest profusion.' On the bowling green stood a maypole decorated with garlands and ribbons, and gaily dressed peasants in old English costume danced around it. 'The company wandered about in the house and garden as they liked; many shot with bows and arrows; others danced under tents, swung, or played all sorts of games, or wandered in the shade of thick shrubberies . . . Many servants were dressed in fancy dresses as gardeners, and garlands of fresh flowers were hung upon all the bushes, which produced an indescribably rich effect.'

A few weeks later he goes to a 'dejeuner champetre' given by the 'Duke of S.' at his villa, 'at which invention was racked for something new in an entertainment of the kind'. The garden was filled with

Cartoon by Henry Heath of the bride Harriot Coutts dancing with her groom, William Aubrey de Vere Beauclerk, 9th Duke of St Albans; Cupid sits on a pile of cash.

sofas, easy chairs, chaise-longues and mirrors with a 'little encampment of tents of white and rose-coloured muslin, which had a beautiful effect, set in the emerald-green of the grounds'. In the evening the garden was lit with lamps in the bushes and trees: 'like so many ruddy fruits or bright glow-worms, enticing the loving or lonely'. There was dancing in a large tent entered through a bowery archway of roses, followed by a concert by performers from the Italian Opera. 'Italian weather, too, happily shone on this fete from beginning to end; any little mischievous spirit of air might have totally ruined it.'

The British weather has always had the last word on the success or failure of the outdoor event, 'if wet in village hall' being an all-too-familiar proviso. The greatest washout in the entire history of such outdoor events must have been the Eglinton Tournament. Planned for 29 August 1839 by the Earl of Eglinton at Eglinton Castle, his Gothic Revival house in Ayrshire, it was to include a mounted grand parade of knights and ladies fully caparisoned in medieval outfits, followed by a tournament. After the earl had invited his friends, he threw the event open to the public: entrance free by prior application for a ticket. He expected four thousand and got nearer to one

The Eglinton Tournament, one of the most disastrous outdoor events ever staged. Viscount Alford and the Marquis of Waterford tried to impale each other, at which point the crowd lost patience.

hundred thousand people, who travelled from all over Britain. As Lady Seymour, dressed as the Queen of Beauty, prepared to lead the parade in glorious splendour, an intense and violent rainstorm reduced the whole ambitious venture to a sea of mud, flood and utter disarray in a couple of hours. The tournament was abandoned but never forgotten.

SHOWING OFF THE GARDEN

Not all garden owners are like John Evelyn, to whom his friend Abraham Cowley, admittedly another passionate horticulturalist, said that he knew of nobody who 'possesses more private happiness than you do in your garden; and yet, no man, who makes his happiness more public, by a free communication of the art and knowledge of it to others'. To be shown round a friend's garden can be a pleasure, but there is a British tendency for the garden tour to become a social weapon. Jane Austen observes this in *Pride and Prejudice,* when Elizabeth Bennett suffers the longueurs of Mr Collins' pride as he

> invited them to take a stroll in the garden, which was large and well laid out, and to the cultivation of which he attended himself. To work in his garden was one of his most respectable pleasures; and Elizabeth admired

Print of 1825 by George Hunt, entitled *The Ne Plus Ultra of Bores,* showing a resigned visitor trailing round the flower beds after a determined female garden enthusiast.

> the command of countenance with which Charlotte talked of the health of the exercise, and owned she encouraged it as much as possible. Here, leading the way through every walk and cross walk, and scarcely allowing them an interval to utter the praises he asked for, every view was pointed out with a minuteness which left beauty entirely behind.

Lady Troubridge's book of etiquette published in 1926 suggests that such a tour was almost a formal obligation and that when friends were invited to tea in the country 'it is usual, if the weather is fine, to ask if they will like to see the garden, for country dwellers are generally interested in gardening'.

This procedure comfortably filled the hour devoted to such a visit.

The American dramatist and monologist Ruth Draper gained numerous fans with her parody *Showing the Garden*, written in the early 1920s. An English lady of advanced middle age guides her visitor into her country garden:

> Come, Mrs. Guffer, do come. I am longing for you to see the garden . . . Tea is not quite ready – and I'm so afraid you are going to run away that I am determined you should have at least a *tiny* glimpse of the garden! I won't take you far . . . Happily it's very near . . . I always feel that I am most fortunate in having a part of my garden into which I can fairly *tumble* . . .
>
> As a matter of fact, you know I am rather sorry you should see the garden now, because alas! it is not looking its best . . . Oh, it doesn't *compare* to what it was last year . . . We've had a very poor season, I think . . . Oh, it's been very much too dry . . . I think everyone has suffered . . .
>
> Next week my *Funnifelosis* should be in bloom . . . They will completely fill that corner that is all bare now with their huge foliage and tall blue blossoms . . . They will make a most lovely mass just there – where it looks rather sad just now, I'm afraid.

So accurately observed were Ruth Draper's words that they are referred to in a description of Sunday lunch at the Frobishers on 1 June 1930 in the *Diary of a Provincial Lady*, which clearly reflected E.M. Delafield's past suffering:

> Weather is wet and cold, and had confidently hoped to escape tour of the garden, but this is not to be, and directly lunch is over we rush out into the damp. Boughs drip on to our head and water squelches beneath our feet, but rhododendrons and lupins undoubtedly very magnificent, and references to Ruth Draper not more numerous than usual. I find myself walking with Mrs. Brightpie (?) who evidently knows all that can be known about a garden. Fortunately she is

prepared to originate all the comments herself, and I need only say, 'Yes, isn't that an attractive variety?' and so on. She enquires once if I *ever* succeeded in making the dear blue Grandiflora Magnifica Superbiensis – (or something like that) – feel really happy and at home in this climate? To which I am able to reply with absolute truth by a simple negative, at which I fancy she looks rather relieved. Is her own life perhaps one long struggle to acclimatise the G.M.S.? and what would she have replied if I had said that, in *my* garden, the dear thing grew like a weed?

On 18 August the Provincial Lady receives another invitation from Lady Frobisher, this time to tea while there is still something to be seen in the garden. '(Do not like to write back and say that I would far rather come when there is nothing to be seen in garden, and we might enjoy excellent tea in peace – so, as usual, sacrifice truth to demands of civilisation.)'

GARDENS FOR CHARITY

It was Miss Elsie Wagg, a member of the council of the Queen's Nursing Institute, who with a flash of genius realized that there was a match to be made between the thousands of people who would happily spend a shilling in going to look round someone else's garden and proud owners who would be happy to open up to the public. So the National Gardens Scheme was started, in 1927, and during the first year 609 gardens were opened and over £8,000 made for district nurses – though a verse called 'Garden Opening' by Caroline Palmer gently pointed out the disadvantages:

> When you open to the public
> They come along and say
> 'Oh what a lovely shrub that is'
> And take a piece away
> They also like to know the names
> Of all the plants on view.
> They never bring a notebook

So they take the labels too.
They like a pretty garden
And expect a damn good tea
And though it's all for charity
Take extra cakes for free.
Because they weren't invited
Inside the house to pass,
You'll find them in the flowerbeds
Their faces to the glass.

Today the National Garden Scheme requires that a garden should have forty-five minutes of interest within its boundaries, so Elsie Wagg's scheme is relatively simple compared to some of the elaborate charity events dreamt up for Victorian and Edwardian gardens, where money was raised to improve the lot of the disadvantaged in society, be they blind, deaf, orphaned, crippled, wounded or fallen (as in women). Throwing open a garden for bazaars, fêtes and parties was an excellent solution to the philanthropic impulse. The lure of access to something exclusive was there for the paying public, but it did not need to involve actually allowing anyone to cross

(Left) Sir Trevor Dawson, armaments manufacturer and managing director of Vickers, throws a garden party at Edgewarebury House, Elstree, 5 July 1930.
(Right) Lord Moynihan opens the Surrey Liberal Association's fête in a Godstone garden, 2 June 1947.

the threshold of the house. No Gothic Revival Victorian vicarage was complete without extensive lawns on which to hold charitable events. The habit remains: even in 2006 suggestions for fund-raising from the Conwy and Denbighshire NHS Trust still included giving a garden party, advising 'unless someone in your group has particularly large garden, organize it in the vicarage garden (with the vicar's agreement)'.

As a conscientious curate Francis Kilvert attended a much-anticipated Hardwick Bazaar for the Home Missions on Monday, 29 August 1870, arriving on the lawn at Hardwick Vicarage at 3.30 p.m. He recorded in his diary:

Miss Hermia Cassell and Lady Flavia Gifford take part in the flowerpot race at a Hampstead garden party in aid of the needy of north St Pancras, 1932.

> The Bazaar was in full swing, the tent very hot and crowded. Everybody was buying everything at once. The Hay Volunteer Band banged and blasted away. Persons ran about in all directions with large pictures and other articles, bags, rugs, cushions, smoking caps, asking everyone they met to join in raffling for them. I bought for 3/6 at the stall of Helen of Troy [Kilvert was deeply susceptible to feminine beauty] a walnut paper knife with a deer carved on the handle by Walwyn Trumper, his first attempt and very nicely done. The entrance to the field over a bridge across the sunk fence from the lawn cost 1/-. At 5 o'clock there was universal tea, cake and bread and butter in a tent with long tables and forms. A pretty dark eyed merry maid waited on us. No teaspoon and I stirred my tea and cut the bread and butter slices with my newly acquired paper-knife.

At 5.30 p.m. the Bishop of Hereford began to speak from the edge of the lawn and did not stop for an hour, and 'the air got very chill towards the end of the Bishop's speech'.

Tory MP Sir William Wayland hooks a bottle of beer at a fête in Chislet, Kent: 2d. a go, the year 1939.

Such events were lengthy affairs and involved sundry committees. A Garden Fête and Sale of Work in aid of the Didsbury Parish Church Alteration Fund was held in 1898 by kind permission of Mr and Mrs Crofton of Manor House. It started at 12.30 p.m., opened by the local MP, and lasted until the band of the 3rd Volunteer Battalion of Manchester Fusiliers played 'God Save the Queen' at nine o'clock in the evening. Amusements included the Great Fish Pond, the Modern 'Aunt Sally', Golf-Putting Competitions and a Bicycle Gymkhana with excellent prizes. Less ambitious, but equally typical, was the 'Bijou Bazaar' advertised 'In the garden at "Southfield," Westbury-on-Trym on Saturday June 15th for the purpose of maintaining a Cot at the Home for Crippled Children for one year. Any gifts of Fancy Articles, Pottery, Paintings or Money, will be gratefully acknowledged by either of the Committee'.

Bicycle gymkhanas were another good idea of Major Walter Wingfield, who had earlier done much to popularize lawn tennis. Lawns were the perfect place to learn to ride the newly popular bicycles, which is probably what inspired him. He introduces his book on the subject, *Bicycle Gymkhana and Musical Rides and Instructions on How to Get Them Up*, with an enthusiastic explosion. 'For the second time in my life I have invented a name! The first time it was "Sphairistike" and no living soul has ever discovered what that name meant!! It is now "Cyckhana," and as it is frequently used in this book; I suppose I must explain it!!!' The cyckhana, for charity or amusement, needed short, well-rolled, level grass, three umpires with two men under them and a list of props which for a twelve-race card included:

4 life-size comic figures, 4 books of telegram forms, 6 Japanese umbrellas, 8 small bouquets, 4 old golf clubs, 6 butterfly nets and 1 dozen tennis balls. He proposed a VC Race (heroically rescuing life-size comic figures), the Siamese Twins (pairs with hands held), Tortoise Race (the slowest) and an Obstacle Race ('Put what obstacles you like, only don't let them be dangerous or unbecoming to the ladies').

The Edwardians, stimulated perhaps by a new century and a new monarch, developed a passion for historical pageants. Performances involved entire towns and villages enacting the complete history of Britain with an appropriately regional slant, and such events lingered on until the Festival of Britain in 1951. One of thousands took place at Enderby in Leicestershire at the Parish Church Garden Fête in June 1928. It opened with

Two small girls inspect a knight in shining armour: Arundel pageant, August 1923.

the lines 'We think that in these days of scurry and bustle it would be as well to take you back for a spell to the quiet days of your forefathers in this village.' After beginning with Hugo de Grentesmesnil, first Norman Governor of Leicester (Mr. K. Barlow), swearing allegiance to William the Conqueror (Mr Alf. Cooper), it progressed via the beheading of Lady Jane Grey – 'this scene is what might have taken place if we had been there to see it' – and ended with a scene of the Victorian Vicar of Enderby preparing for a temperance meeting in 1868, and a minuet danced by Misses Toon and Jibbs with Mr A. Neale.

Virginia Woolf wrote a parody of a pageant in *Between the Acts*, published posthumously in 1941. In aid of installing light in the village church and held on the terrace at Pointz Hall, the pageant is organized by the ambitiously artistic Miss La Trobe.

Everyone was clapping and laughing. From behind the bushes issued Queen Elizabeth – Eliza Clark, licensed to sell tobacco. Could she be Mrs Clark of the village shop? She was splendidly made up. Her head, pearl-hung, rose from a vast ruff. Shiny satins draped her. Sixpenny brooches glared like cats' eyes and tigers' eyes; pearls looked down; her cape was made of silver – in fact swabs used to scour saucepans. She looked the age in person.

'The prettier the scene, the more truly pleasing the surroundings and outlook, the more certainly successful will be the entertainment . . . lawns are almost indispensable, if only from the point of view of picturesqueness,' states *The Fête & Amusement Organisers' Handbook*, published after the First World War. The charities are those helping the 'maimed, widows and orphans', and everyone is encouraged to discover How To Play the Good Samaritan. It gives instructions on committees, advertising and publicity; programme sellers ('it need not be emphasized that the ladies – and next to them the smartest boys and girls – make the best sellers), organizing the teas ('unless these items are skilfully organized, the worst kind of chaos and dissatisfaction may ensue'), bicycle parking (twopence, sixpence for a motor bicycle) and music ('quite indispensable and if you are able to secure a local "military" band so much the better') are all covered in helpful detail. Possible side shows are listed: Aunt Sally, Topping the Topper, Hoop-la, Cocoa-Nut [sic] Shies, Shooting Galleries, Grass Billiards, 'Jazz' Bagatelle, Bucket

The jumble stall doing brisk business in a vicarage garden: Chislet fête in 1939. The charge was 6d. per item.

Quoits, the Fish Pond and the Weighing Chair, as well as Lawn and Garden Competitions for Everybody which include Hat Trimming for Men ('it will be strange if the products of their labours do not keep every girl and woman present in roars of laughter'), Needle and Cigarette Race ('supremely funny' – men thread needles and women light cigarettes), Bolster Fights, Flowerpot Race, Whiskey and Soda Race ('in view of the cost of the drinks provided, the entrance fee will have to be rather larger than for your ordinary competitive events').

Raise Cash – Have Fun was the 1969 successor to this book; Cancer Research and the local youth club were suggested charities, but the enthusiasm was identical: 'I firmly believe that raising money can be an adventure, offering a splendid opportunity for enriching the lives of all those who are generous and sympathetic and energetic enough to take the plunge!' Apart from the fête, it says, the summer garden could be put to good use with alternatives such as an informal Brunch Party one summer Sunday morning that could be held on a small patio or garden lawn with deck chairs, hammocks, lots of cushions 'and a general air of relaxation'. This could be followed up with a Quoit Tennis Tournament 'to keep the party in full swing'.

E.M. Delafield's Provincial Lady predictably has to host a fête:

> Entire household rises practically at dawn, in order to take part in active preparations for Garden Fete. Mademoiselle reported to have refused breakfast in order to put final stitches in embroidered pink satin boot-bag for Fancy Stall, which she has, to my certain knowledge, been working at for the past six weeks. At ten o'clock our Vicar's wife dashes in to ask what I think of the weather, and to say that she cannot stop a moment.
>
> ... Lady Frobisher arrives – ten minutes too early – to open Fete, and is walked about by Robert until our Vicar says, Well, he thinks perhaps that we are now all gathered together ... (Have profane impulse to add *'In the sight of God'*, but naturally stifle it.)
>
> Lady F. is poised gracefully on the little bank under the chestnut tree, our Vicar beside her, Robert and myself modestly retiring a

few paces behind, our Vicar's wife kindly, but mistakenly, trying to induce various unsuitable people to mount bank – which she humorously refers to as the Platform – when all is thrown into confusion by sensational arrival of colossal Bentley containing Lady B. – in sapphire-blue and pearls – with escort of fashionable creatures, male and female, apparently dressed for Ascot.

'Go on, go on!' says Lady B., waving hand in white kid glove, and dropping small jewelled bag, lace parasol, and embroidered handkerchief as she does so. Great confusion while these articles

At Flaunden in Hertfordshire, the village fête committee count the proceeds.

are picked up and restored, but at last we do go on, and Lady F. says what a pleasure it is to her to be here to-day, and what a desirable asset a Village Hall is, and much else to the same effect . . . – someone else thanks Robert and myself for throwing open these magnificent grounds – (tennis-court, three flower borders and microscopic shrubbery) . . . Lady B. spends ninepence on a lavender bag, and drives off again with expensive-looking friends . . .

Band arrives, is established on lawn, and plays selections from *The Geisha* . . . Robert has information, no doubt reliable, but source remains mysterious, to the effect that we have Cleared Three Figures. All, for the moment, is *couleur-de-rose*.

10 A PLACE FOR BIRDS AND BEASTS

Gardens have always offered space for both strictly practical and more frivolous engagement with animals. Smallholdings are not gardens, but gardens have frequently had aspects of smallholdings. Naturally, animal husbandry has the longer history: the poor old widow living in a small cottage with her two daughters in Chaucer's *Nun's Priest's Tale* used her garden traditionally by being simply self-sufficient with three sows, three cows, a sheep called Molly, Chanticleer the cock and seven hens, including the incomparable Lady Pertelote. They lived on hard work, milk, bread, bacon and eggs. Producing food for the family table might be an emergency measure, as it was for Nella Last, a middle-aged housewife living in Barrow-in-Furness in Lancashire. Only a day after the Second World War was declared she wrote in her Mass Observation diary:

> My husband laughs at me for what he terms 'raving', but he was glad to hear of a plan I made last crisis and have since polished up. It's to keep hens on half the lawn. The other half of the lawn will grow potatoes, and cabbage will grow under the apple trees and among the currant bushes. I'll try and buy this year's pullets and only get six, but when spring comes I'll get two sittings and have about twenty extra hens in the summer to kill. I know a little about keeping hens and I'll read up. My husband just said 'Go ahead'.

A Ministry of Information photograph of Mrs Brown and her daughter Peggy feeding the chickens in their garden at Rowney Green, Worcestershire, during the Second World War.

Exotic fauna, too, have been nurtured, played with and displayed for a long time. Animals and their needs keep a garden used and enjoyed almost as much as plants.

A PLACE FOR PRACTICAL ANIMALS

Tending poultry was generally the woman's role. The poultry were kept close to the house and fed partly on scraps from the kitchen, and advice on how to do this best has always been copious. In *The Suburban Gardener and Villa Companion* of 1838 J.C. Loudon lists suitable animals for keeping in gardens from fifty feet in length upwards. He gives instructions for the best construction of hen houses – which could be ingeniously heated with a pipe of hot water running out of the house from a cistern at the back of the kitchen fire – fowl-fattening houses, turkey houses and pigeon houses. Pigeons, he said, were unsuited to small gardens, since they would be always raiding the neighbour's garden vegetables; however, the following were fine: rabbits, edible snails – to be kept in large pits covered with boards and fed cabbage leaves – and even large green frogs, kept in ponds and 'fed for culinary purposes, as it is in France, Germany and Italy'. A

mid-nineteenth-century compendium of occupations for boys suggested that they might keep domestic fowl ('the pleasure of the occupation is considerably enhanced by the visions it conjures up of new-laid eggs and yellow custards, and fine, plump smoking fowls'), with the advice that if profit was the motif, look no further than a Dorking. The very slight *Handbook of Profitable Hobbies* – 'turn your spare hours into spare cash' – dating from between the two world wars suggests 'Rabbits as a Paying Proposition', 'When Poultry Breeding Pays', 'Dog Rearing for Cash and Kudos', 'Live Stock that More Than Repays its Keep', 'Cage Birds and Pigeons for Private Profit' and 'Bees and Honey bring you Money'.

The reality of animals in the garden, of course, had a downside, as Charles Dickens reported on Agar Town in the magazine *Household Words* (1851): 'Every garden had its nuisance . . . In one was a dung-heap, in the next a cinder-heap, in a third, which belonged to the cottage of a costermonger, was a pile of whelk and periwinkle shells, some rotten cabbages, and a donkey.' The dung heap was a constant feature of an equivalent country dwelling in agriculturally depressed late nineteenth-century Oxfordshire, as described by Flora Thompson in *Lark Rise to Candleford*: 'At the back or side of each cottage was a lean-to pigsty and the house refuse was thrown on a nearby pile called "the muck'll". This was so situated that the oozings from the sty could drain into it; the manure was also thrown there when the sty was cleared, and the whole formed a nasty, smelly eyesore to have within a few feet of the windows.'

APIARIES

Bees had a double role in the garden: a practical one as honey providers and pollinators, and an exemplary one as the paradigm of industry for mankind.

Loudon's Bayswater beehive, illustrated in *The Suburban Gardener*, 1838.

In his 1677 gardening manual John Worlidge pointed out that 'Idleness is so detestable a vice among them, that they will not admit it, nor tolerate it, any (save the sovreign) but everyone is continuously busied, either abroad in collecting their food, or at home in building combs, feeding their young, or some other employment.' Lessons were meant to be drawn: 'their labour is not compulsive, everyone acting his part voluntarily, and seemingly contend and endeavour to outvie each other in their nimble expeditious voyages, when they so mightily lade themselves, that many times their decayed wings are not able to support them home.' William Mew, Rector of Eastington in Gloucestershire, designed a beehive set with a small pane of glass through which the bees could be watched; this his wife thoughtfully had built for him while he was away from home during the Civil War. The pattern was passed on to John Evelyn, who showed it to Charles II who, Evelyn reported, contemplated it with much satisfaction.

Two hundred years later the architect J.B. Papworth made precisely the same point in *Hints on Ornamental Gardening* about his design for an ornamental apiary with a glass back: 'few studies afford more satisfactory results to persons of leisure and reflection, than are to be obtained by contemplating the habits and conduct of these little animals from which just lessons of prudence, industry, and social virtue, may be as correctly acquired, as from deep-studied instructions of the schools.' J.C. Loudon placed his bees under the veranda of his Bayswater house. They were protected from rain and sun and he claimed that when the back of the hive was opened the bees could be conveniently examined at work. He used the new type of Nutt's hive, an important development that allowed the honey to be harvested without killing the bees.

Of course the study of bees' industry could be hazardous, as the diarist Francis Kilvert found:

> After tea Mrs. Bridge took us round into the garden to show us her hives. One bee instantly flew straight at me and stung me between the eyes, as I was poking about the hives in my blind way [he had awful eyesight]. I did not say anything about it and Mrs. Bridge congratulated me on my narrow escape from being stung. All the while the miserable bee was buzzing about entangled in my beard, having left his sting between my eyes. Consequently I suppose he was in his dying agony. Then we walked round the garden and along the water walk, while the water ran out of my eyes.

Bees were highly valued by Queenie, an elderly and impoverished lace maker whose relationship with her hives Flora Thompson describes in *Lark Rise to Candleford*. On sunny days Queenie sat beside her beehives, working at pillow lace or dozing in the shadow of her lilac sunbonnet. She was guarding against losing a swarm:

When at last, the long-looked-for swarm rose into the air, Queenie would seize her coal shovel and iron spoon and follow it over the cabbage beds and down the pea-stick alleys, her own or if necessary, other peoples', tanging the spoon on the shovel: *Tang tangtangety-tang!*

She said it was the law that, if they were not tanged, and they settled beyond her own garden bounds, she would have no further claim to them . . . So she would follow and leave her shovel to mark her claim, then go back for her long green veil and sheepskin gloves to protect her face and hands while she hived her swarm.

When her husband died she was seen knocking on the roof of each hive in turn, saying, "'Bees, bees, your master's dead, an' now you must work for your missis'" and explaining, "'I 'ad to tell 'em, you know or they'd all've died, poor cratars.'"

The best-selling *Life of the Bee* by Maurice Maeterlinck, which came out in 1901, inspired yet another generation of amateur beekeepers for whom bees were not merely useful insects but something more significant. The authoress Marion Cran gushed in *The Garden of Ignorance* (1913) dramatically of his inspiration, which led her to order a colony of bees from Welwyn, and how thanks to Maerterlinck the 'buzzing box' was transformed for her into a 'mystery palace where a wondrous queen and indefatigable virgins and the splendid lazy knights of love' live in her garden.

MENAGERIES

Whimsical animal keeping has a long history. Medieval European monarchs and princes sought to outdo each other in the keeping and giving of exotic animals from distant countries. They seemed to be playing God and attempting to create prelapsarial gardens of Eden adjoining their palaces. In the eleventh century Henry I had a menagerie at his palace at Woodstock with lions, leopards, porcupines, camels and 'strange spotted beasts' from 'diverse outlandish lands'.

Many garden owners with space, money and enthusiasm created

buildings worthy of their animals. Discussing the ornamental aspects of a garden, Henry Wotton in his 1624 book *Elements of Architecture* suggests 'Conservatories of rare Beasts, Birds, and Fishes'. As ever the Victorians were eclectic in their choice of architectural style, and J.C. Loudon illustrates designs for kennels in Italianate, Tudor or Gothic style in his *Encyclopedia of Cottage, Farm and Villa Architecture*, 1883. Shortly afterwards, George Durant of Tong in Shropshire selected an Egyptian theme for a stone pyramid pigsty on which he had inscribed 'To Please the Pigs'. His twenty-foot-high henhouse was of similar shape and apparently carved with such exhortations as 'Teach your Granny' and 'Scratch before you Peck'. From the same period is a miniature classical temple over a pool that John Evelyn's descendants built at Wotton House in Surrey for some much-loved terrapins.

Full-blown menageries were conspicuously ostentatious affairs. Lord Halifax commissioned one for his Northamptonshire estate at Horton, combined it with a banqueting house and filled it with raccoons, a couple of tigers, eagles, ermine and various fancy birds. If the owner lost interest, the prospect was clearly less enchanting. When Prince Pückler-Muskau inspected the garden at Chiswick House in October 1826, he found that the menagerie there, established by the 6th Duke of Devonshire after he had inherited the house in 1811, had giraffes, kangaroos and emus to amuse visitors, but Pückler-Muskau felt that it had gone decidedly off – stagnant slimy water, more black earth than green foliage – and he was underwhelmed by a tame elephant performing all sorts of feats 'that very quietly suffers anybody to ride him about a large grass-plat. His neighbour is a lama, of a much less gentle nature; his weapon is the most offensive saliva, which he spits out to a distance of some yards at any one who irritates him; he takes such good aim, and fires so suddenly at his antagonist, that it is extremely difficult to avoid his charge.'

A town garden was no bar to having an exotic collection of animals. The anatomist Joshua Brookes at least had reason to keep animals in his garden in Blenheim Street in London, since for forty years he ran the Brookesian Museum of Comparative Anatomy. One may suspect that his famous Vivarium, which could be viewed by curious passers-by in the street through a grille, contained a few animals awaiting their fate on the dissecting table. There was a raccoon, a chained eagle, an egret and a tortoise that inhabited a 'Rock of Gibraltar' structure of a rather cyclopean nature with niches and perches; water from a spout in a stone crocodile head poured into a giant

Engraving of Joshua Brookes's garden after a drawing by George Scharf, 1830.
The arch of the 'pilgrim's cell' to the right was made from the jaw bones of a whale,
and had a stained-glass rose window.

clamshell. It is recorded that panicking bystanders mobbed the house when a nearby fire at the Pantheon in Oxford Street saw the animals frantically trying to escape.

The Duke of Devonshire's Chiswick elephant comes down through the years as a melancholy beast and many other exotic animals outlived their novelty value and mouldered, forgotten, to spend a sad old age penned up in a British garden. The Victorian artist Daniel Gabriel Rossetti had a taste for collecting animals that were 'quaint, odd or semi-grotesque', which he kept at Cheyne Walk in Chelsea during the 1860s. His brother William listed them in his memoir, with the comment 'persons who are familiar with the management of pets will easily believe that several of these animals came to a bad end': there was a Pomeranian puppy named Punch (got lost), a grand Irish deerhound named Wolf (inadequately exercised and given away), a barn owl named Jessie, another owl named Bobby, rabbits, dormice (fought, killed one another, ate their own tails and gradually perished), hedgehogs, two successive wombats, a Canadian marmot, or woodchuck, an ordinary marmot, armadillos (burrowed into next-door house and caused the cook to think it was a visitation from the Devil), kangaroos, wallabies, a deer, a white mouse with her brood, a raccoon, squirrels, a mole, peacocks, wood owls, Virginian owls, Chinese horned owls, a jackdaw, laughing jackasses, undulated grass parakeets (neglected while Rossetti was away and died), a talking grey parrot, a raven, chameleons, green lizards and Japanese salamanders. Another failure was his purchase of a zebu (or small Brahmin bull) that had to be speedily resold after it went 'into hostile mood', probably, it was agreed, as a result of being tied permanently to a tree. As William Rossetti laconically added: 'this experience showed that

Rossetti's sketch of himself mourning the death of his wombat 'Top', which he described as sweet and fat.

the zebu was not a convenient tenant for the garden.' The screeching of the peacocks so infuriated Rossetti's neighbour and landlord, Lord Cadogan, that he inserted a clause in all Cheyne Walk leases forbidding the keeping of peacocks. The artist finally gave the peacock away after his deer had systematically trampled on all its tail feathers and destroyed its appeal.

Even if inconveniently large and eye-catching bird species such as peacocks and pheasants were beyond the capacity of many gardens, it was quite acceptable to round up smaller wild ones and keep them in captivity, with the aim of filling your garden with the sound of birdsong. The early seventeenth-century author William Lawson writes in *A New Orchard and Garden* of obtaining 'a brood of nightingales, who with their several notes and tunes, with a strong delightsome voice, out of a weake body, will bear you company night and day'. Francis Bacon disliked aviaries unless, he wrote in his essay 'Of Gardens', they were large enough to 'have living plants and bushes set in them; so that the birds may have more scope for natural nestling, and that no foulness appear in the floor of the aviary'. Lady Henrietta Luxborough

Elegant oriental-style pheasantry designed by Repton for the Prince Regent at Brighton Pavilion, 1808.

thought the aviary an essential garden feature for her Hertfordshire house and wanted one for the birdsong, writing in a letter, 'I have made a garden which I am filling with all the flowering shrubs I can get. I have also made an aviary, and filled it with a variety of singing birds, and am now making a fountain in the middle of it, and a grotto to sit and hear them sing in contiguous to it.'

The Boy's Own Book lists possible pets for the Victorian child. First on the list is singing birds to hang in the window, which could be enjoyed by those with little or no garden at all; but first they had to be caught. 'There are few men who do not remember with pleasure the day they first made the House-sparrow prisoner in the common brick trap; or – if they have been greater adepts, when boys, in the art of bird-catching – the moment when they first saw the Finch leg-fast to their lime-twig, a few fine Larks safe in their net, a Thrush noosed in a springle of their own construction.' Nightingales could be caught by luring them with mealworm, but were delicate and needed careful looking after. 'As soon as you have taken the nest, place it in a small basket, and cover it up warm, for they are very susceptible of cold, and will soon die if exposed to it. Begin to feed them on small caterpillars or fresh ants' eggs, mixed with a small portion of white bread, grated and moistened.'

More exotic birds demanded exotic surroundings and aviaries were frequently glamorous buildings. When Robert Dudley, Earl of Leicester, famously entertained Queen Elizabeth at Kenilworth Castle for nineteen long days in 1575, he had an aviary. This was described by a contemporary observer, possibly with hyperbole, as being ornamented with gilt and studded with diamonds, emeralds, rubies and sapphires. The birds made 'melodious music', holly trees were planted at either end and there were roosting spots in the wall for the birds to be either cool or warm to be broody; with marble pilasters, sumptuously painted and gilded, the aviary was twenty feet high and thirty feet long.

There was still enthusiasm for strange birds with eye-catching plumage two hundred years later. 'I saw an ostrich walking in the lawn near the house,' wrote Richard Pococke in his travel diary of the Duke of Cumberland's garden in 1754. Caroline Lybbe Powys was very engaged in the subject and indeed built her own aviary 'on the site of the old Wilderness Walk' in her garden at Fawley in Oxfordshire. In 1764 she was much entertained by the bird collection at Bulstrode in Buckinghamshire belonging to the Dowager Duchess of Portland, describing it in her diary as the 'finest in England – curassoa, goon, crown-bird, stork, black and red games, bustards, red-legg'd partridges, silver, gold, pied pheasants, one what is reckon'd exceedingly curious, the peacock-pheasant.' No aviary, however, was as spectacular as the one she saw in 1796 when visiting General Owen Williams at his new house called Temple, near Marlow, which she likened to a palace in an Arabian Nights' entertainment. 'At the farther end of the most magnificent greenhouse is an aviary full of all kinds of birds, flying loose in a large octagon of gilt wire, in which is a fountain in the centre, and in the evening 'tis illuminated by wax-lights, while the water falls down some rock-work in form of a cascade. This has a pretty effect, but seems to alarm its beautiful inhabitants, and must be cold for them I should imagine.'

Of the birds in the menagerie at Osterley she thought the situation dreary and unpleasant, and 'the menagerie, which for years I had heard so much of, fell far short of my expectation.' Yet fifteen years earlier, in June 1773, Horace Walpole in a letter to the Countess of Upper Ossory had described the *nouveaux riches* improvements made by the banker Sir Francis Child: 'a palace of palaces! – and yet a palace *sans crown, sans coronet*; but such expense! such taste! such profusion! . . . all the Percies and Seymours of Sion must die of envy' and amongst it all 'a menagerie full of birds that come from a thousand islands that Mr. Banks has not discovered'.

Prize card for Grey Dawn, a racing pigeon bred and raced in Norwich.

Selective bird breeding appears to have appealed mainly to the male mind. Flemish weavers in Norwich had specialized in canaries bred for their singing and bright yellow, and back-garden bird fanciers of the nineteenth century bred pigeons into Frillbacks, Spanish Runts, Parisian Pouter, Uploper, Trumpeter, Jacobines, Finikins and Ermine or Bald-Pated Tumblers. Pigeons had also been bred as messengers after it was discovered that they could carry news of everything from political events to Derby winners extremely fast, but this use came to an end with the advent of the telegraph, so instead pigeon fanciers turned to competitive pigeon racing. Lofts were built in back yards and gardens, on roofs and on allotments all over Britain, becoming particularly popular in working-class areas and in mining communities. A south Wales miner has described how there were four or five pigeon lofts in the back gardens of each street, with about thirty birds apiece in the period after the First World War; and Robert Roberts' study of Salford during the same period reports on the uses of back yards: 'Father cobbled and mended there, kept a rabbit or two, pigeons (common indeed) or a few hens.'

The Royal Society of Birds was created in the 1860s to save the great crested grebe from being hunted to extinction to meet the demands of milliners who wanted their plumes for hats. Attitudes were changing and rather than collecting birds' eggs and keeping wild birds in cages people were encouraged to lure birds into their garden and then just observe them. Bird tables and bird baths popped up in thousands of gardens. By the time that the 1945 King Penguin *Garden Birds* was published there was a sophisticated menu system in place: kipper skins were relished by starlings; mutton fat was for tits and hemp seed for finches; and sunflower seeds were irresistible to greenfinches.

The song of wild birds became part of the BBC's first outside broadcast after the musician Beatrice Harrison, practising her cello at night in her Oxted cottage garden during the 1920s, discovered, to her astonishment, that the nightingales started singing as she played. Inspired by the thought of making this extraordinary duet available to city-dwellers and the gardenless everywhere, she persuaded Lord Reith to transmit it on the wireless. Thus one evening in May 1924 she put on full evening dress and played some Elgar and Dvorak, while her summer house was crammed full of anxious BBC sound technicians. The Savoy Orpheans were ousted from their customary Saturday evening slot and the recording began. Finally, to the relief of all involved, the nightingales obliged with song during the last fifteen minutes of the programme. The world listened, Miss Harrison was overwhelmed with letters of appreciation and the BBC reprised the programme from her garden for the next twelve years.

The neighbourhood cats gather malevolently
at the sound of Beatrice Harrison and the nightingale emitting
from a suburban couple's wireless: *Punch* cartoon by Arthur Watts, 1933.

AND OTHER PETS

The idea of keeping animals as pets would have astonished many of our ancestors, for whom an animal was simply a food source, just as they would have been astonished at the idea of good soil being used simply for decorative flowers and trees. By Victorian times the range of possible pets was extensive. Loudon lists among animals that could be kept in suburban gardens 'for those who wish to add to their sources of recreation and amusement': tortoises, tree frogs 'either in a cage as an ornament or in the greenhouse as a useful fly-catcher' or silkworms (eggs available in Covent Garden Market during May and June). *The Boy's Own Book* contributed another suggestion: 'No little animal lays claim to more admiration, or is a greater favourite amongst boys, than the Squirrel. In domestication it soon becomes tame, and the playfulness and vivacity of its nature are rendered more attractive by the affection it displays towards its protector. Although not equal to a dog, it may be taught to perform a variety of amusing little tricks.' Kilvert's friend Mrs Hocking 'has two pet toads, which live together in a deep hole in the bottom of a stump of an old tree. She feeds them with breadcrumbs when they are at home, and they make a funny little plaintive squeaking noise when she calls them. Sometimes they are from home

A NOVEL EXPERIMENT.
"WHAT ON EARTH ARE YOU DOING WITH THE CRUET-STAND?"
"OH, WE'RE ONLY OILING THE JOINTS OF THE TORTOISE. IT MOVES ALONG SO STIFFLY, POOR THING!"

George du Maurier's cartoon on keeping tortoises for an 1883 edition of *Punch*.

especially in the evenings.' The 'Home Pets' chapter of *Cassell's Book of Sports and Pastimes*, however, was disparaging about toads as pets: 'certainly a tame toad demands a deal of trouble for very little, except the curiosity of the thing'. Tortoises, too, were dismissed as not having the intelligence to show real attachment, but good garden material since they hibernated in winter and foraged for themselves in summer. On the subject of a hedgehog the book is more enthusiastic, if quiet on the subject of fleas: 'he does to some extent repay petting, for he always gets to know the one that feeds him, and will put down his bristles and allow himself to be stroked by that one at least, sometimes even licking the hand and making a queer attempt at play.'

Guinea pigs 'are amusing little animals and may be kept in a small house with a little yard to run about in', wrote Loudon, implying a detachment not felt by Charles James Saville Montgomerie Lamb, who in 1823 began at the age of seven to create a miniature medieval city, which he dubbed Winnipeg, for his pet guinea pigs. Their extensive castle-hutch was complete with battlements, keeps, archways and flying flags. Each animal was given a coat of arms that was recorded in their history, written and illustrated by Charles in miniature volumes. Writing home from boarding school, he asked his mother to supervise the erection of a tombstone to Cavy, the first queen of the castle. He was consistent in his interests, as he was a major player in the Eglinton Tournament described in the previous chapter, giving himself the title of Knight of the White Rose.

The guinea pig castle in the garden at Beauport near Littlehampton in Sussex.

The invention of the cat flap gave the domestic cat – and occasionally dog – the freedom of the garden. The architect M.H. Baillie Scott, in his book *Houses and Gardens*, written in 1906, explains how 'the demands' of family pets could be met in what was an increasingly suburbanized world by building a small passage made through the wall or chimney breast provided with self-closing doors hung from the upper edge, which the animals – and this included dogs – would soon learn to push open. In the twentieth century the inevitability of pet ownership led the garden designer John Brookes reluctantly to address the aesthetic problem of hutches and huts in *Room Outside*: 'In many households there tends, at a certain stage, to be a need for pets: rabbits, guinea pigs, etc. In my own home, in addition to the family dog, we seem to have had, in quick succession, a magpie, rabbits, white mice, and a mallard hatched by a bantam hen!' He said that pets' housing was very unattractive 'unless very well organised' and should be screened.

Other people's pets have frequently been a source of desperation for their neighbours. In 1777 William Curtis in *Flora Londinensis* wrote about the 'serious annoyance' caused by cats. The Carlyles were neighbours of the Rossettis in Chelsea, and certainly might have complained about the noise of Rossettis' peacocks. For all Thomas's life he struggled with a neurotic hatred of noise – cocks and pianos in particular – and their Chelsea years were punctuated by disputes with neighbours over bird noises from adjoining gardens. Jane wrote despairingly, 'Cocks are springing up more and more, till it seems as if the Universe were growing into one poultry yard.' Parrots and macaws were highly fashionable pets in mid-Victorian suburban circles and although they lived inside during summer their large cages were moved into the garden. The Lambert family next door to the Carlyles had one such parrot, which drove Carlyle to declare that he could 'neither think nor live'. Subsequent neighbours, an Irish family called Ronca, were even more troublesome, since they kept both cockerels and a macaw called Sara. It took a £5 payment by Carlyle to buy his peace and they were eventually legally bound never to keep either fowls or macaws again.

Birds screeching from gardens is also a theme of the mid-nineteenth century. *The Semi-Detached House*, Emily Eden's novel set in the London suburb of Dulham, includes this passage:

'Got a headache, Charles?'

'One ache more or less makes little difference to me. I ought to have a headache. Have none of you found out who owns that dreadful macaw? It has been screaming all day.'

Now it is a remarkable fact in natural history that in all the suburbs of London, consisting of detached houses, called by auctioneers 'small and elegant' or on Terraces described as first-rate dwellings, there always is an invisible macaw, whose screaming keeps the hamlet or terrace in a constant state of irritation.

Today the Neighbours From Hell in Britain website ('an online internet community helping people deal with, manage and resolve neighbour problems') has a special section: 'All About Dog Noise and Barking'.

IN MEMORIAM

At the end of every pet's life comes death and the gardens of Britain, large and small, are littered with memorials to beloved animals. When Horace Walpole looked at the Temple of British Worthies erected by Lord Cobham at Stowe he was upset by the inclusion of monuments to the still-living Alexander Pope and Sir John Barnard and, in a letter of May 1765, reasoned, 'I will not place an ossuarium in my garden for my cat, before her bones are ready to be placed in it.' Walpole had cats called Fanny, Mufti and Ponto – but he does not specify which one was to be honoured with an ossuarium. Richard Pococke was impressed by a horse tomb at Marston in Somerset: 'In one part of the garden a very fine horse of my Lord's is buryed with a monument – a pedestal, with an urn, I think, on it; on three sides, in English, there is an account of the horse, and on the fourth side is this latin inscription, "Hic sepultus est Rex Nobby Equorum Princeps omnium sui generis longe praestantissimus obiit Feb. 12, 1754, Aetat 35."'

When Lord Byron inherited the vast and semi-derelict Newstead Abbey in Nottinghamshire, seeking company he evidently inhabited it with a quantity of recherché livestock, including a tame bear, a wolf and a number of tortoises. He took great pleasure in the company of his dogs and frequently swam in the lake with them. The distress he felt when his favourite Newfoundland, Boatswain, died of rabies in 1808 was acute and he wasted no time in erecting a large monument in the garden, on the exact spot where he believed the high altar of the original priory on the site had been. The lengthy poem cut into the marble is impassioned. Not only does it describe the dog as having

> . . . Beauty without Vanity
> Strength without Insolence
> Courage without Ferocity
> And all the Virtues of Man without his Vices

but Byron is also outraged that the dog, 'The Firmest Friend', is

> Denied in heaven the soul he had on earth
> While man, vain insect, hopes to be forgiven
> And claims himself a sole exclusive heaven.

While the following verses hardly reach Byronic heights, the animals nonetheless inspired garden memorials. One noted in a Shropshire garden a terrier named Scruffy:

> Scruffy
> If his bladder had been stronger
> He would have lived a good deal longer

In the garden of a cottage in Blockley in Gloucestershire a tame trout has a memorial, with a verse to commemorate twenty years of communication between it and William Keyte at the edge of his garden pond, which finally ended in 1855:

> Under the soil
> The old fish do lie
> 20 years he lived
> And then did die
> He was so tame
> You understand
> He would come and
> Eat out of our hand.

For adults stone monuments and poetry are probably sufficient, but for children the ritual of a garden burial is important, as Nancy Mitford, recalling her own childhood, captures in her novel *The Pursuit of Love* (1945). Fanny, the narrator, has just announced that a mouse called Brenda has died. She admits to herself that her 'honeymoon days with the mouse were long since over; we had settled down to an uninspiring relationship', but her cousin Linda minds more:

Views on pet death and burial expressed by the Weber family in Posy Simmonds' 1985 cartoon, originally published in *The Guardian*.

'Where is she buried?' Linda muttered furiously, looking at her plate.

'Beside the robin. She's got a dear little cross and her coffin was lined with pink satin.'

'Now Linda darling,' said Aunt Sadie, 'if Fanny has finished her tea why don't you show her your toad?'

SELECT BIBLIOGRAPHY

Adburgham, Alison, *View of Fashion*, London, 1966

Alexander, A., *Healthful Exercises for Girls*, London, 1902

Anstruther, Ian, *The Knight and the Umbrella: An Account of the Eglinton Tournament*, London, 1963

Aubrey, John, *Brief Lives*, ed. Oliver Lawson Dick, London, 1949

Baillie Scott, M.H., *Houses and Gardens*, London, 1906

Batsford, Harry and Fry, Charles, *The English Cottage*, London, 1938

Birkin, Andrew, *J.M. Barrie and the Lost Boys*, London, 1979

Boorde, Andrew, *The Wisdom of Andrew Boorde*, abridged version of *The Dyetary of Helth*, ed. H. Edmund Poole, Leicester, 1936

Boy's Own Book, London, 1855

Broad, Richard, and Fleming, Suzie (ed.), *Nella Last's War: A Mother's Diary 1939–1945*, Bristol, 1981

Brock, Alan, *A History of Fireworks*, London, 1949

Brookes, John, *Room Outside*, London, 1969

Brown, Jane, *The Pursuit of Paradise: A Social History of Gardens and Gardening*, London, 1999

Brown, Richard, *Domestic Architecture*, London, 1842

Brownell, Morris R., *Alexander Pope and the Arts of Georgian England*, Oxford, 1978

Butler, E.M. (ed.), *A Regency Visitor: The English Tour of Prince Puckler-Muskau Described in his Letters, 1826–1828*, from the original translation by Sarah Austin, London, 1957

Burney, Frances (Mme d'Arblay), *The Early Diary of Frances Burney, 1768–1778*, ed. Annie Raine Ellis, vol. I, London, 1889

Carpenter, Humphrey, *Secret Gardens: A Study in the Golden Age of Children's Literature*, London, 1985

Child, L.M., *The Girl's Own Book*, London, 1876 (enlarged edition 'considerably enlarged and modernized by Mrs. L. Valentine')

Church, Thomas, *Gardens are for People*, San Francisco, 1955

Coffin, David R., 'Venus in the Eighteenth-Century English Garden', *Garden History*, vol. 28, winter 2000

Cowper, William, *Life & Letters*, ed. William Hayley, London, 1835

Cran, Marion, *The Garden of Ignorance*, London, 1913

Crathorne, James Cliveden, *The Place and the People*, London, 1995

Crathorne, James, *The Royal Crescent Book of Bath*, London, 1998

Crispin, T., *The English Windsor Chair*, Stroud, 1992

Daniel, Samuel, *The Complaynt of Fair Rosamond*, Edinburgh, 1887

Davidson, Caroline, *A Woman's Work is Never Done: A History of Housework in the British Isles, 1650–1950*, London, 1982

Darley, Gillian, *John Evelyn: Living for Ingenuity*, London, 2007

Davis, John, *Antique Garden Ornament*, Woodbridge, 1999

Delany, Mrs, *The Autobiography and Correspondence of Mary Granville, Mrs. Delany*, ed. Lady Llanover, 3 vols, 1861

Dodsley, R., *A Description of the Leasowes, the Seat of the Late William Shenstone*, London, 1780

Draper, Ruth, *The Art of Ruth Draper*, London, 1960

Fagg, Christine, *Raise Cash – Have Fun*, London, 1969

Felton, S., *Gleanings on Gardens*, London, 1897

Fort, Tom, *The Grass is Greener: Our Love Affair with the Lawn*, London, 2000

Felus, Kate, 'Boats and Boating in the Designed Landscape, 1720–1820', *Garden History Society*, vol. 34, no. 1, summer 2006

Gardiner, Juliet, *Wartime: Britain 1939–1945*, London, 2004

Gilbert, Christopher, *English Vernacular Furniture, 1750–1900*, Connecticut, 1991

Gillmeister, Heiner, *Tennis: A Cultural History*, London and Washington, 1997

Godfrey, Walter H., *Gardens in the Making*, London, 1914

Gothien Marie Luise, *A History of Garden Art*, London, 1928

Grigson, Geoffrey, *Gardinage*, London, 1952

Henry, Warren, *The Fete & Amusement Organiser's Handbook*, London, n.d.

Hadfield, Miles, *Gardens of Delight*, Cassell, London, 1964

Hardyment, Christina, *Dream Babies: Child Care from Locke to Spock*, London, 1983

Harris, John, *A Garden Alphabet*, London, 1979

Harwood, T. Eustace, *Windsor Old and New*, London, 1929

Heathcote, J.M., *Tennis, Lawn Tennis, Rackets and Fives (Badminton Library of Sports and Pastimes)*, London, 1890

Henderson, Paula, *The Tudor House & Garden*, London, 2005

Hentzer, Paulus, *Travels in England during the Reign of Queen Elizabeth*, ed. Sir Robert Naunton, London, 1894

Hervey, George F., and Hems, Jack, *The Book of the Garden Pond*, London, 1958

Hill, Rosemary, *Stonehenge*, London, 2008

Holme, Thea, *The Carlyles at Home*, Oxford, 1965

Horn, Pamela, *Victorian Country Women*, Oxford, 1991

Hughes, John Arthur, *Garden Architecture and Landscape Gardening*, London, 1866

Hunt, John Dixon, *The Oxford Book of Garden Verse*, Oxford, 1993

Hunt, John Dixon, and Willis, Peter (eds.), *The Genius of Place: the English Landscape Garden, 1620–1820*, London, 1975

Jacobson, Dawn, *Chinoiserie*, London, 1993

Jekyll, Gertrude, *Wall and Water Gardens*, London, 1901

—, *Children & Gardens*, London, 1908

—, and Weaver, Lawrence, *Gardens for Small Country Houses*, London, 1913

Jellicoe, Sir Geoffrey, Jellicoe, Susan, Goode, Patrick, Lancaster, Michael (ed.), *The Oxford Companion to Gardens*, Oxford, 1986

Johnes, Martin, 'Pigeon-Racing and Working Class Culture in Britain, *c.*1870–1950', *Cultural and Social History – The Journal of the Social History Society*, 4:3, 2007

Johns, Revd C.A., *Gardening for Children*, London, 1848

Jones, Barbara, *Follies & Grottoes*, London, 1953

Kilvert, Revd, *Francis Kilvert's Diary: Selections from the Diary of the Rev. Francis Kilvert*, vols I and 2, ed. William Plomer, London, 1938, 1939

King, Anthony D., *The Bungalow*, London, 1984

Kurrein, Carol, *The Flymo Book of Garden Games and Leisure*, Newton Abbot, 1989

La Rochefoucauld, François de, *A Frenchman in England, 1784, Being the Melanges sur l'Angleterre of F. de L.R.*, Cambridge, 1933

Lambton, Lucinda, *Beastly Buildings*, London, 1985

Langley, Batty, *New Principles of Gardening*, London, 1723

Laurence, John, *The Clergyman's Recreation*, 1714, 2nd edition

Lawson, William, *A New Orchard and Garden*, London, 1618

Longstaffe-Gowan, Todd, *The London Town Garden, 1740–1840*, London, 2001

Lorris, W., and Clopinel, J., *The Romance of the Rose, englished by F.S. Ellis*, London, 1900

Loudon, J.C., *Encyclopedia of Cottage, Farm and Villa Architecture*, London, 1833

—, *The Suburban Gardener and Villa Companion*, London, 1838

Loudon, Mrs, *The Lady's Country Companion; or How to Enjoy a Country Life Rationally*, London, 1845

Luxborough, Henrietta, *Letters Written by the Late Right Honourable Lady Luxborough to William Shenstone Esq.*, London, 1775

MacCarthy, Fiona, *William Morris: A Life for our Time*, London, 1994

Markham, Gervase, *Countrey Contentments, or The English Huswife*, London, 1623

Mawson, Thomas, *The Art and Craft of Garden Making*, London, 1926

Miles, Eustace, *The Eustace Miles System of Physical Culture*, London, 1907

Miller, Naomi, *Heavenly Caves: Reflections on the Garden Grotto*, London, 1982

Morgenthau Fox, Helen, *Patio Gardens*, New York, 1929

Morris, Christopher (ed.), *The Journeys of Celia Fiennes*, London, 1949

Mowl, Timothy, *Gentlemen and Players*, Stroud, 2000

Muthesius, Hermann, *Das englische Haus*, 1908, transl. *The English House*, London, 1979

Muthesius, Stefan, *The English Terraced House*, London, 1982

Nichols, Beverley, *Down the Garden Path*, London, 1932

—, *Sunlight on the Lawn*, London, 1956

Oliver, Paul, Davis, Ian, and Bentley, Ian, *Dunroamin*, London, 1981

Orme, N., *Early British Swimming*, Exeter, 1983

Papworth, J.B., *Hints on Ornamental Gardening*, London, 1823

Pepys, Samuel, *The Diary of Samuel Pepys*, ed. with additions by Henry B. Wheatley, vol. 5, London, 1895

Pococke, Dr Richard, *Travels through England*, ed. James J. Cartwright, Camden Society volume, London, 1888

Raverat, Gwen, *Period Piece*, London, 1952

Repton, H., *Sketches and Hints on Landscape Gardening*, London, 1794

—, *Fragments on the Theory and Practice of Ornamental Gardening*, London, 1816

Richards, J.M., *The Castles on the Ground*, London, 1973

Richardson, Tim, *The Arcadian Friends*, London, 2007

Roberts, Robert, *The Classic Slum: Salford Life in the first Quarter of the Century*, Manchester, 1971

Robinson, William, *The English Flower Garden*, London, 1883

Rogers, Pat, *The Oxford Illustrated History of English Literature*, Oxford, 1987

Rogers, W.S., *Villa Gardens*, London, 1902

Rohde, Eleanour Sinclair, *The Old-World Pleasaunce*, London, 1925

Ross, Noel, *The House-Party Manual*, London, 1917

Ross, Stephanie, *What Gardens Mean*, Chicago, 1998

Rossetti, Dante Gabriel, *His Family Letters, with a Memoir by Michael Rossetti*, volume I, 1895

Scott-James, Anne (with Osbert Lancaster), *The Pleasure Garden*, London, 1977

Sedding, John D., *Gardencraft Old and New*, London, 1891

Sinclair, Archibald, and Henry, William, *Swimming (Badminton Library of Sports and Pastimes)*, Longmans, 1908

Strong, Roy, *The Renaissance Garden in England*, London, 1979

Strutt, Joseph, *The Sports and Pastimes of the People of England*, London, 1867

Switzer, Stephen, *Ichonographia Rustica: or the Nobleman, Gentleman and Gardener's Recreation*, London, 1742

Taylor, Gordon, and Cooper, Guy, *Gardens of Obsession*, London, 1999

Temple, Sir William, *Upon the Gardens of Epicurus, with other XVIIth Century Garden Essays*, introduction by Albert Forbes Sieveking, London, 1908

Tinniswood, Adrian, *The Polite Tourist: A History of Country House Visiting*, London, 1998

Tunnard, Christopher, *Gardens in the Modern Landscape*, London, 1938

Turner, R.C., 'Mellor's Gardens', *Garden History: The Journal of the Garden History Society*, vol. 15, autumn 1987

Walker, Penelope, and Crane, Eva, 'The History of Beekeeping in English Gardens', *The Journal of the Garden History Society*, vol. 28, winter 2000

Walpole, Horace, *The Letters of Horace Walpole, Fourth Earl of Orford*, ed. Paget Toynbee, Oxford, 1903–5

Ware, Isaac, *The Complete Body of Architecture*, London, 1756

Waters, Michael, *The Garden in Victorian Literature*, London, 1988

Watton, James (ed.), *The Faber Book of Smoking*, London, 2000

Weaver, L. (ed.), *The House and its Equipment*, London, 1911

Weightman, Gavin, and Humphries, Steve, *The Making of Modern London 1815–1914*, London, 1983

Williamson, Tom, *Polite Landscapes*, Stroud, 1995

Woodbridge, Kenneth, *The Stourhead Landscape*, London, 2002

Woods, May, *Visions of Arcadia: European Gardens from Renaissance to Rococo*, London, 1996

Wordsworth, Dorothy, *The Journals*, ed. Mary Moorman, Oxford, 1971 (text copyright © Dove Cottage Trust)

TEXT ACKNOWLEDGMENTS

Every effort has been made to trace copyright holders. Any we have been unable to reach are invited to contact the publishers so that a full acknowledgment may be made in subsequent editions. The author and publishers are grateful to the following for permission to reproduce copyright material:

John Betjeman, 'The Subaltern's Love Song', *Collected Poems*, reproduced by permission of John Murray (Publishers)

Elizabeth Bowen, *Friends and Relations*, reproduced with permission of Curtis Brown Group Ltd, London, on behalf of the Estate of Elizabeth Bowen. Copyright © Elizabeth Bowen 1931

Richmal Crompton, *The Family Roundabout*, reproduced by permission of A.P. Watt Ltd on behalf of Dr Paul Ashbee.

Ruth Draper, *The Art of Ruth Draper*, reproduced by permission of Doubleday, New York

Aldous Huxley, *Crome Yellow*. Copyright © Aldous Huxley. Reprinted by permission of Georges Borchardt, Inc., for the Estate of Aldous Huxley

Laurie Lee, *Cider with Rosie*, reprinted by permission of PFD on behalf of the Estate of Laurie Lee, © Laurie Lee, 1959

Excerpt from *Pursuit of Love* by Nancy Mitford (© Nancy Mitford 1945) is reproduced by permission of PFD (www.pfd.co.uk) on behalf of the Estate of Nancy Mitford

P.G. Wodehouse, *Crime Wave at Blandings* and *If I Were You*. Copyright © P.G. Wodehouse, reproduced by permission of the Estate, c/o Rogers, Coleridge & White Ltd, London

Virginia Woolf, *Between the Acts*, reproduced by permission of the Society of Authors as the Literary Representative of the Estate of Virginia Woolf